JUNIOR CYCLE SPHE
THIRD YEAR

YOU'VE GOT THIS!

BOOK 3

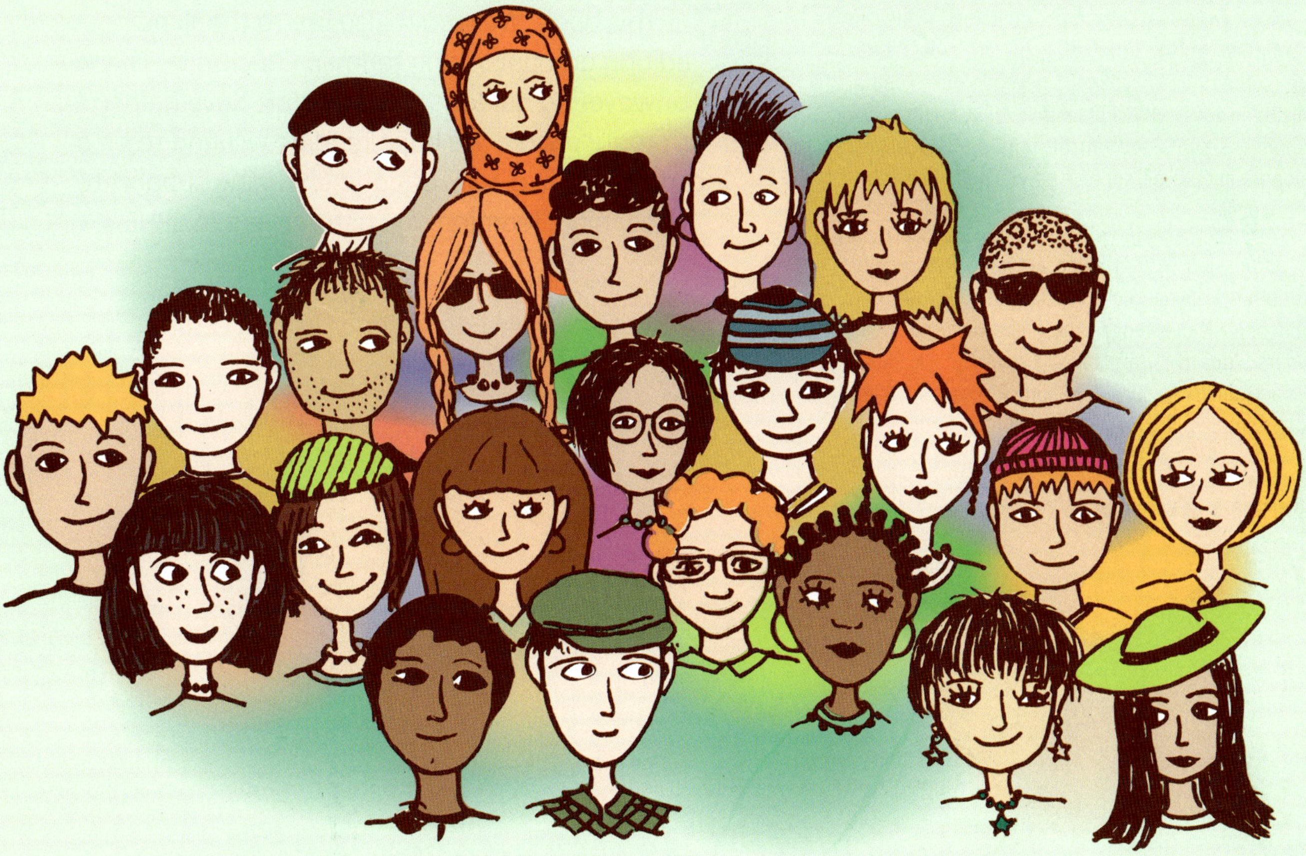

Genevieve Cooney and Denise Dalton

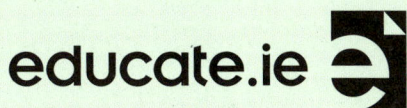

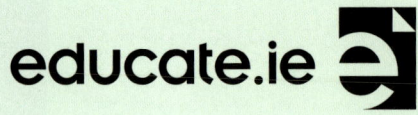

PUBLISHED BY:
Educate.ie
Walsh Educational Books Ltd
Castleisland, Co. Kerry, Ireland
www.educate.ie

PRINTED AND BOUND BY:
Walsh Colour Print, Castleisland, Co. Kerry, Ireland

Copyright © Genevieve Cooney and Denise Dalton, 2024

Without limiting the rights under copyright, this book is sold subject to the condition that it shall not, by way of trade or otherwise, be reproduced, stored in or introduced into a retrieval system, or transmitted, in any form or by any means (electronic, mechanical, photocopying, recording or otherwise), or otherwise circulated, without the publisher's prior consent, in any form other than that in which it is published and without a similar condition, including this condition, being imposed on the subsequent publisher.

Weblinks were active and contained relevant information at the time of going to press. URLs and content may change beyond our control. Educate.ie does not accept responsibility for the views or opinions contained on the third-party websites. Students should be supervised when visiting third-party websites.

For permission to reproduce artwork, photographs and other copyrighted material, the authors and publisher acknowledge the following copyright holders: dpa picture alliance / Alamy Stock Photo; Michael Cullen / Alamy Stock Photo; PA Images / Alamy Stock Photo; Photoshot / TopFoto; Shutterstock

ISBN: 978-1-915595-94-2

Acknowledgements

We would both like to thank our families and close friends, who were patient, supportive and encouraging throughout the process of writing this book. We would also like to thank our editing and publishing team in Educate.ie. Their unwavering guidance and support have helped us produce what we hope readers will find to be a comprehensive, relevant and engaging support to teaching, learning and assessment in SPHE.

Genevieve Cooney and Denise Dalton

Contents

Introduction v

Information for Teachers viii

| Unit 1 | Understanding My Thoughts and Actions .... 1 |

Chapter 1	Tracing My Past, Understanding My Present, Picturing My Future 2
Chapter 2	Intrinsic and Extrinsic Motivation 8
Chapter 3	Understanding Personality Types 13
Chapter 4	Bias, Inequality and Exclusion 18
Chapter 5	Diversity and Inclusion 23
Chapter 6	Mistakes, Criticism and Self-Compassion 29
Chapter 7	Kindness 36
Chapter 8	The Science of Happiness 41

| Unit 2 | Caring for My Mind and Body .... 46 |

Chapter 9	What Is Within and Beyond Our Control? 47
Chapter 10	Mastering Resilience in Challenging Times 52
Chapter 11	Coping Tools to Enhance Resilience 58
Chapter 12	Building a Positive Relationship with Food 63
Chapter 13	Disordered Eating Behaviours 67
Chapter 14	The Effects of Edited Images 73

| Unit 3 | Understanding and Dealing with Substance Use .... 78 |

Chapter 15	Problematic Substance Use 79
Chapter 16	Addiction 83
Chapter 17	Substance Use: What Influences Our Choices? 89
Chapter 18	Substance Use and Peer Pressure 95
Chapter 19	Positive Coping Strategies 101

Unit 4	Intimate Relationships	106
Chapter 20	The Role of Intimacy and Pleasure in Relationships	107
Chapter 21	Consent in Intimate Relationships	111
Chapter 22	Pressures to Become Sexually Intimate	116
Chapter 23	Popular Culture and Sexual Expression	121
Chapter 24	What Is Pornography and Why Is It a Concern?	125
Chapter 25	The Impact of Pornography	129
Chapter 26	Ending Relationships	134

Unit 5	Sexual and Emotional Wellbeing	144
Chapter 27	Sexual Harassment	145
Chapter 28	The Influence of Social Media on Gender Norms	150
Chapter 29	Contraception: Options and Communication	156
Chapter 30	Contraception: Making Choices	160
Chapter 31	STIs: Transmission and Types	165
Chapter 32	STIs: Testing and Treatment	170

Introduction

Welcome to your Third Year Junior Cycle SPHE course. We hope that you enjoy using *You've Got This! – Book 3* on your learning journey.

You've Got This! – Book 3 textbook
Key features

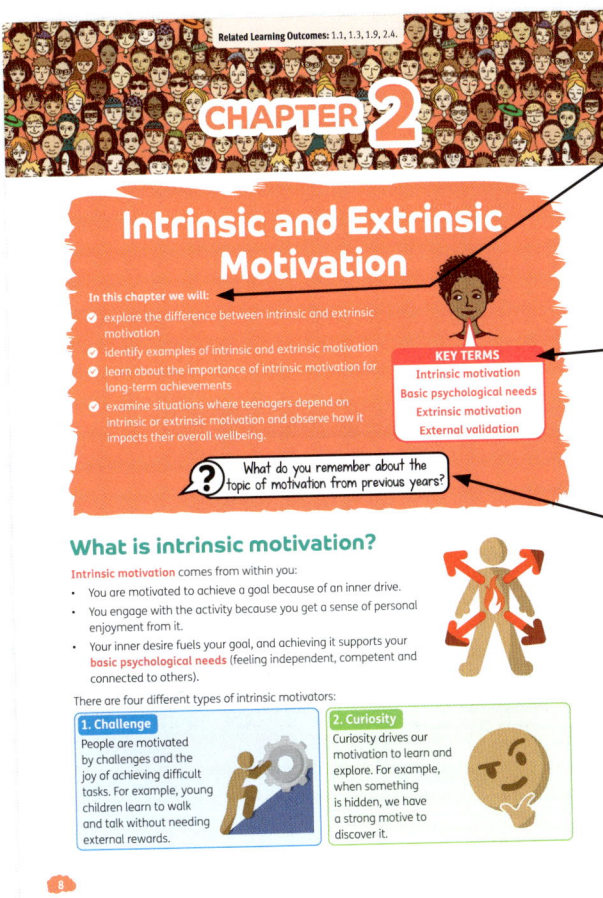

Chapters open with **learning intentions** to let you know what you will cover in the chapter.

Key terms are listed at the start of each chapter and are highlighted in the text.

An **opening question** gets you thinking about the chapter topic.

Individual, pair-work and group-work **activities** are presented under clear action headings:

THINK   CREATE
DISCUSS WATCH
READ   ROLE PLAY

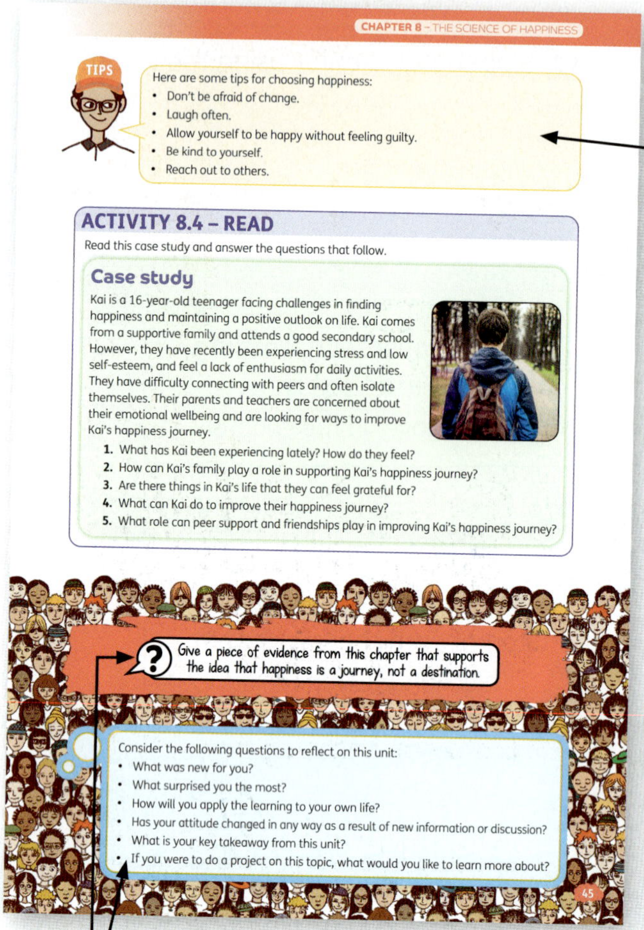

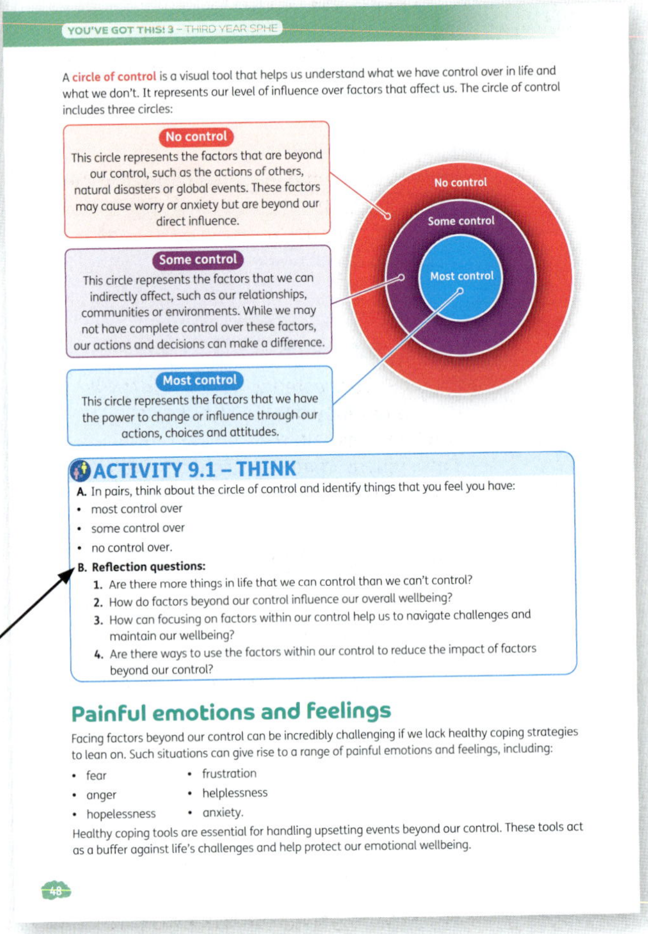

YOU'VE GOT THIS! 3 – THIRD YEAR SPHE

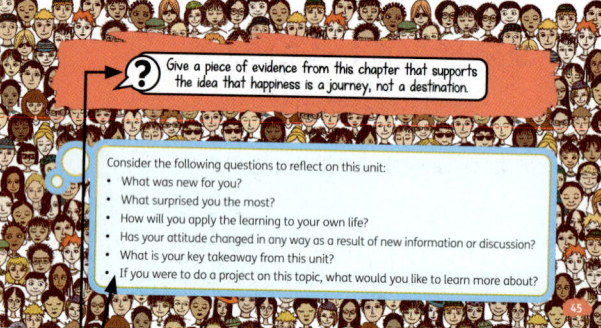

Tip boxes appear throughout the textbook to give you practical advice and support.

Closing questions at the end of each chapter and end-of-unit **reflection questions** give you the opportunity to assess and reflect on where you are in your learning journey.

Many activities have **reflection questions**.

Icon key

 Opening and closing questions

 Pair work

 Group work

 Link to online video

 Option to complete activity on the *You've Got This!* app

 Activity can contribute to 'Portfolio of my learning and my reflection on SPHE' CBA option

 Activity can contribute to 'Taking action for SPHE' CBA option

Key Skills

You will use the Junior Cycle Key Skills when you are completing the activities in *You've Got This! – Book 3*.

Indicators of Wellbeing

You've Got This! – Book 3 supports you in developing the Indicators of Wellbeing.

ACTIVE
- Am I a confident and skilled participant in physical activity?
- How physically active am I?

RESPONSIBLE
- Do I take action to protect and promote my wellbeing and that of others?
- Do I make healthy eating choices?
- Do I know where my safety is at risk and do I make right choices?

CONNECTED
- Do I feel connected to my school, my friends, my community and the wider world?
- Do I appreciate that my actions and interactions impact on my own wellbeing and that of others, in local and global contexts?

RESILIENT
- Do I believe that I have the coping skills to deal with life's challenges?
- Do I know where I can go for help?
- Do I believe that with effort I can achieve?

RESPECTED
- Do I feel that I am listened to and valued?
- Do I have positive relationships with my friends, my peers and my teachers?
- Do I show care and respect for others?

AWARE
- Am I aware of my thoughts, feelings and behaviours and can I make sense of them?
- Am I aware of what my personal values are and do I think through my decisions?
- Do I understand what helps me to learn and how I can improve?

You've Got This! app

You've Got This! comes with a free app that can be used to complete some of the activities in the textbook. Visit **www.educateplus.ie/sphe-1-app** for more details.

You've Got This! – Book 3 digital resources

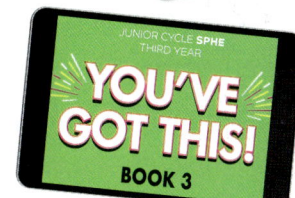

Digital resources including an ebook are available at:
www.educateplus.ie/resources/sphe-3

Information for Teachers

Thank you for choosing *You've Got This! – Book 3* to teach Third Year Junior Cycle SPHE. Please note that chapters have been designed to be covered in single lessons, or can be easily adapted to cater for a school's specific SPHE timetable.

You've Got This! – Book 3 and the Junior Cycle SPHE specification

You've Got This! – Book 3 has been written for the new SPHE specification and RSE requirements. The Junior Cycle SPHE specification sets out a course of learning that is spread across four strands.

Across these four strands there are 39 Learning Outcomes that indicate the learning and skills that students should have acquired over the course of their Junior Cycle SPHE journey.

In *You've Got This! – Book 3*, Learning Outcomes have been carefully selected and grouped together in chapters. Chapters have then been grouped into units of learning. Learning Outcomes addressed in a chapter are listed at the very start of the chapter:

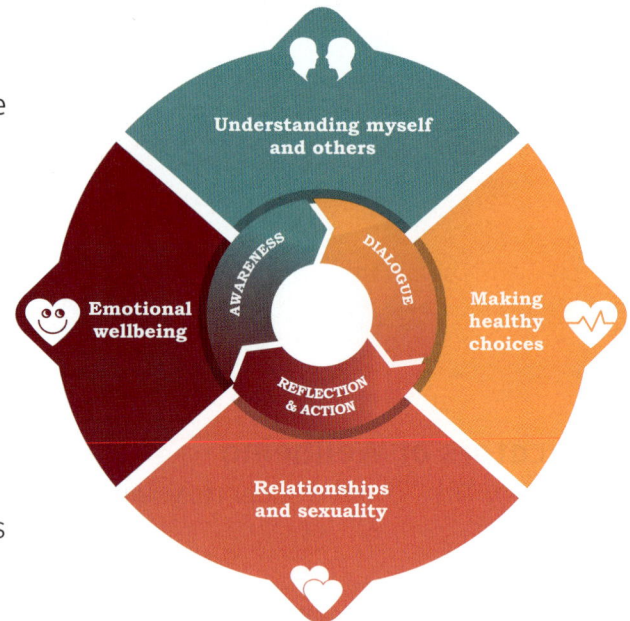

It is important to note that *You've Got This! – Book 3* follows a non-linear, spiral approach to the Learning Outcomes, where students meet and revisit Learning Outcomes at appropriate times. This means that Learning Outcomes listed at the start of each chapter may be only partially covered. Students will revisit these Learning Outcomes later in their Junior Cycle course. All Learning Outcomes will be fully covered by the time students complete their three-year Junior Cycle course.

You've Got This! Teacher's Resource Book

The comprehensive Teacher's Resource Book provides extensive information to support you in teaching SPHE. It contains:

- information on the new specification and Learning Outcomes
- guidance on planning and sample plans
- background information on key topics based on the latest research and data
- explanations on active learning methodologies/pedagogical approaches
- comprehensive information on possible responses students may share in class
- suggested responses for teachers to support effective facilitation of lessons
- guidance on using the *You've Got This!* app
- teambuilding and communication activities with links to demonstration videos
- templates and strategies.

UNIT OF LEARNING 1

Understanding My Thoughts and Actions

The chapters in this Unit of Learning are:
- Chapter 1 – Tracing My Past, Understanding My Present, Picturing My Future
- Chapter 2 – Intrinsic and Extrinsic Motivation
- Chapter 3 – Understanding Personality Types
- Chapter 4 – Bias, Inequality and Exclusion
- Chapter 5 – Diversity and Inclusion
- Chapter 6 – Mistakes, Criticism and Self-Compassion
- Chapter 7 – Kindness
- Chapter 8 – The Science of Happiness

Note for teachers: This Unit of Learning engages with the following Learning Outcomes:

1.1 explore the physical, social and emotional changes that happen during adolescence
1.2 reflect on their personal strengths and values and how they bring these into relationships
1.3 explore the range of influences and life experiences that can impact on self-image and self-esteem and identify ways to nurture a positive sense of self-worth
1.4 recognise the factors and influences that shape young people's self-identity, such as family, peers, culture, gender identity, sexual orientation, race/ethnic background, dis/abilities, religious beliefs/world-views
1.6 discuss experiences/situations of bias, inequality or exclusion and devise ways to actively create more inclusive environments
1.7 communicate in a respectful and effective manner and listen openly and sensitively to the views/feelings of others
1.8 reflect on the meaning and importance of empathy and discuss ways that it can be expressed
1.9 demonstrate self-management skills, including setting personal goals, delaying gratification, and self-regulation of thoughts, emotions and impulses
2.4 demonstrate skills and strategies to help make informed choices that support health and wellbeing and apply them in real-life situations that may be stressful and/or involve difficult peer situations
4.1 discuss the fluid nature of emotional wellbeing and ways to nurture and protect it
4.4 discuss ways to support themselves and others in challenging times and where/how/when to seek support, if needed

Related Learning Outcome: 1.9.

CHAPTER 1

Tracing My Past, Understanding My Present, Picturing My Future

In this chapter we will:
- pause and reflect on our growth and achievements over the last two years
- look towards our future goals and dreams
- consider a goal we have and discuss how to achieve it.

KEY TERMS
Aspirations
Milestones

? As you begin your third year of secondary school, what are the top three emotions or feelings that you are experiencing?

Time to pause and reflect

We often find ourselves so caught up in the present moment that we fail to take time to pause and reflect on our past. Looking back on what we've learned helps us to understand our growth. It's like a personal rewind – we see our mistakes, celebrate our wins and find ways to do better.

CHAPTER 1 – TRACING MY PAST, UNDERSTANDING MY PRESENT, PICTURING MY FUTURE

ACTIVITY 1.1 – CREATE

This exercise aims to help you appreciate your journey, recognise your strengths and identify areas for improvement.

A. Reflect on the last two years since you started secondary school. You might want to focus on:
- major events
- new things you've learned, such as how to make new friends or be more independent
- joining a sports team
- dealing with a big argument with a friend
- starting a relationship.

B. Create a timeline of these events and lessons. This timeline template can be used.

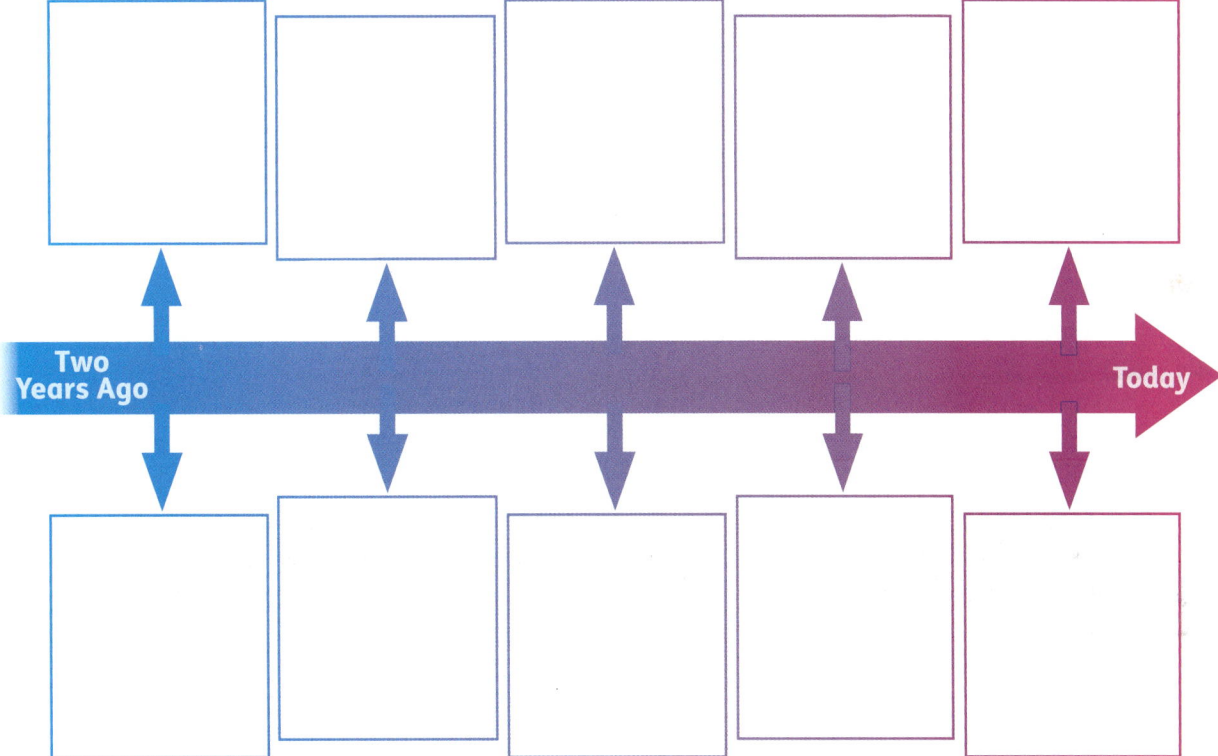

C. Reflection questions:
1. What significant events occurred?
2. What were some of the challenges you faced and how were they overcome?
3. What new skills or knowledge were gained?
4. What are you most proud of from the past year?

Picturing your future

Now that you're in Third Year, you might begin to picture your future more often. What vision do you have of your future? What are your goals and aspirations? Goals are clear targets we work towards within a specific time, while **aspirations** are our broader dreams and desires for the future (e.g. to pursue a career in medicine in order to improve people's health and save lives).

YOU'VE GOT THIS! 3 – THIRD YEAR SPHE

Looking towards your future is like drawing a roadmap for your dreams. It makes you excited to work towards your goals, which may include:

- making new friends
- achieving the Junior Cycle Profile of Achievement
- becoming more resilient
- earning your own money
- developing a healthy romantic relationship.

Having a vision for your future:

- gives you direction
- helps you make decisions today that will lead you to where you want to be tomorrow
- is very motivating – when things get tough, remembering your future goals can help you keep going.

Research shows that your big dreams can have as much, or even more, impact on your life's achievements as things like your intelligence (IQ) or your family's financial status.

Let's have a look at some people who dared to dream big as teenagers and have succeeded in life, despite facing countless obstacles. Each of them showed unwavering commitment and resilience on their journey to success.

Lionel Messi

Lionel developed a passion for sport from an early age, joining his first football club at four years old. His dream of being a professional footballer was threatened when he was diagnosed with a growth hormone deficiency at age 10. Despite facing financial difficulties, his family relocated to Spain to provide him with access to better medical treatment and football opportunities. After successful treatment, and through sheer determination, talent and hard work, Lionel rose above his challenges to become one of the greatest football players in history.

Taylor Swift

From a young age, Taylor had ambitious dreams of becoming a music star. She faced early rejections in Nashville, but persevered. Her unique storytelling ability, resilience and adaptability to different genres has led her to huge success, making her one of the most influential artists of her generation.

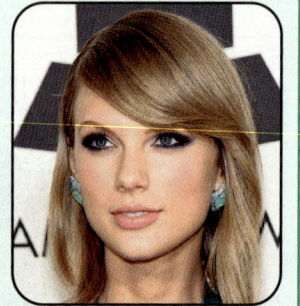

Barry Keoghan

Barry, an Irish actor, achieved his dreams through hard work and dedication. Despite experiencing personal and financial difficulties in his youth, he pursued his passion for acting and gradually began making a name for himself in the industry. His commitment to his craft has led to his success in film and television.

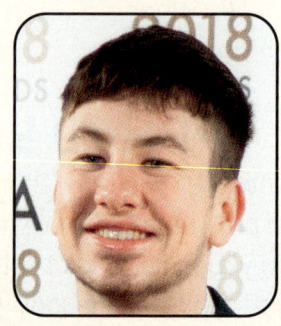

CHAPTER 1 – TRACING MY PAST, UNDERSTANDING MY PRESENT, PICTURING MY FUTURE

Malala Yousafzai

As a teenager, Malala fought for girls' education in Pakistan. She faced significant adversity, including a life-threatening attack by the Taliban. After surviving a gunshot wound, she continued her mission of advocating for education rights, winning the Nobel Peace Prize at age 17.

Greta Thunberg

As a teenager, Greta dreamt of a world where climate change was taken seriously. She started protesting alone and sparked a global movement to reduce the effects of climate change. She has been mocked and criticised for her actions, with many people discounting her ideas because of her age. However, Greta has shown that one young person can make a huge difference.

Peter Dinklage

Peter, an actor, has proven that talent and determination can lead to success. Born with dwarfism, Peter encountered obstacles in the entertainment industry due to limited opportunities for actors with disabilities. With his exceptional performances in various films and TV shows, he has become an inspiration, breaking barriers in the entertainment industry.

Sean McLoughlin

Sean, also known as Jacksepticeye, is a prominent YouTuber who has built a massive following through his entertaining and energetic video game commentary. Despite struggling with his mental health and burnout, he persisted in pursuing his passion, ultimately becoming an influential figure in the online gaming community.

Katie Taylor

Born in Bray, Co. Wicklow, Katie faced adversity due to the lack of support and infrastructure for women's boxing in Ireland. Nevertheless, she became an Olympic gold medalist and a two-weight world champion, making her one of the most successful female boxers of all time.

These inspiring people didn't achieve success overnight. It took hard work and a belief in themselves to get them where they are today. Think about other people in your life who inspire you. Is there anything you can learn from them?

ACTIVITY 1.2 – WATCH

Watch this video of Cristiano Ronaldo speaking about his successes and answer the questions that follow.

 www.educate*plus*.ie/go/cristiano-ronaldo

1. What does Cristiano repeatedly tell himself?
2. What two things do you need to improve, according to him?
3. What does Cristiano say is his main strength?
4. 'Records is part of me. I don't follow the records. The records follow me.' What do you think he means by this?

ACTIVITY 1.3 – READ

In pairs, read these two case studies and answer the questions that follow.

Case study 1

Chloe feels unsure about her future goals and aspirations. She doesn't have a clear vision of what she wants to pursue in life, and feels overwhelmed by the pressure of deciding what subjects to take in Senior Cycle. She enjoys playing basketball and the piano, but these activities don't spark a strong passion or sense of purpose in her. She often finds herself comparing herself to her peers who seem to have their goals figured out.

1. Can you relate to the experience of feeling uncertain about your goals and aspirations? How does it make you feel?
2. How could you handle the pressure of not knowing your goals while seeing other people have a clear direction?
3. What steps can Chloe take to explore different interests and discover her passions?

> 'My goal is not to be better than anyone else, but to be better than I used to be.' – Wayne W. Dyer

Case study 2

Kevin is passionate about gaming. He dreams of becoming a professional gamer and making a living doing what he loves. Kevin spends hours practising and following his favourite players online. As a result, he often neglects his schoolwork, believing that his gaming skills alone will lead him to success. He doesn't see the value in working hard at school because he views gaming as his ultimate goal in life.

1. Can you understand Kevin's passion for gaming and his desire to become a professional gamer?
2. What are some potential drawbacks or challenges Kevin may face by neglecting his schoolwork?
3. How can Kevin balance his passion for gaming with his schoolwork?

> 'A goal without a plan is only a wish.' – Antoine de Saint-Exupéry

CHAPTER 1 – TRACING MY PAST, UNDERSTANDING MY PRESENT, PICTURING MY FUTURE

Achieving future goals

In order to achieve our future goals, we need to plan for them. This can involve breaking them down into:

- **Milestones**: These are stages or events that we reach or complete while working towards a goal.
- **Projects**: These are activities we can do to help us achieve a goal.
- **Tasks**: These are actions we can do to help us reach a goal.

Breaking goals down into these smaller stages allows us to stay on track on our journey to future success.

ACTIVITY 1.4 – CREATE

Think about a big goal you want to achieve in your life. This can be related to:

- school life
- relationships
- your future career
- personal development.

Break this goal down into milestones, projects and tasks. An example has been done for you below. Remember, there are no right or wrong ideas, and everyone's aspirations are valid and important. (Note: You can look back on your notes from Activity 2.2, page 8 of *You've Got This! – Book 2* to see your goals from Second Year.)

GOAL
Improve physical fitness and achieve a healthy lifestyle

MILESTONE
Successfully complete a 5 km run within the next six months.

PROJECT
Create a personalised fitness plan and follow it consistently for three months.

TASK
Incorporate healthy eating habits by including more fruits and vegetables in meals.

TASK
Work with a fitness professional to design a personal exercise routine. Set specific targets for weekly workouts.

TASK
Keep a fitness journal to track progress, note achievements and identify areas for improvement.

? Look back at your goals from last year. Have you achieved any of them, or even successfully progressed them in some way?

Related Learning Outcomes: 1.1, 1.3, 1.9, 2.4

CHAPTER 2

Intrinsic and Extrinsic Motivation

In this chapter we will:
- ✓ explore the difference between intrinsic and extrinsic motivation
- ✓ identify examples of intrinsic and extrinsic motivation
- ✓ learn about the importance of intrinsic motivation for long-term achievements
- ✓ examine situations where teenagers depend on intrinsic or extrinsic motivation and observe how it impacts their overall wellbeing.

KEY TERMS
Intrinsic motivation
Basic psychological needs
Extrinsic motivation
External validation

 What do you remember about the topic of motivation from previous years?

What is intrinsic motivation?

Intrinsic motivation comes from within you:
- You are motivated to achieve a goal because of an inner drive.
- You engage with the activity because you get a sense of personal enjoyment from it.
- Your inner desire fuels your goal, and achieving it supports your **basic psychological needs** (feeling independent, competent and connected to others).

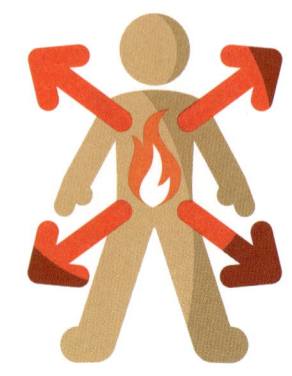

There are four different types of intrinsic motivators:

1. Challenge
People are motivated by challenges and the joy of achieving difficult tasks. For example, young children learn to walk and talk without needing external rewards.

2. Curiosity
Curiosity drives our motivation to learn and explore. For example, when something is hidden, we have a strong motive to discover it.

8

CHAPTER 2 – INTRINSIC AND EXTRINSIC MOTIVATION

3. Control

Having a sense of control over our environment is naturally motivating. It allows us to feel empowered and to take action. For example, a teenager who decides to start their own band takes control of the creative process, selecting the band members and choosing the songs to play.

4. Context

Learning becomes more meaningful when it relates to real-life situations and goals. By understanding how skills are relevant and useful, we boost our inner motivation to learn and improve. For example, learning a new language can feel challenging, but when you realise that knowing the language can help you communicate with people from different cultures, travel to new places or even enhance your career opportunities, the relevance and usefulness of the skill become clear.

What is extrinsic motivation?

Extrinsic motivation comes from external factors:
- You are motivated to achieve a goal because you want a reward in return.
- You engage with an activity because you are focused on an outcome.
- External gains fuel your goal (e.g. money, fame, power, avoiding consequences).

There are three different types of extrinsic motivation:

1. Reward-based motivation

This type of motivation comes from external rewards, such as prizes or benefits. For example, a person may post on Instagram because they want to receive likes and comments.

2. Power-based motivation

Power-based motivation comes from the desire to control or influence others. For example, a student may run for a student council position because they desire the authority to make decisions and influence school policies.

3. Fear-based motivation

Fear-based motivation comes from the desire to avoid negative consequences or punishments. For example, a student might study hard for an upcoming exam because they fear receiving a low grade, which could result in disappointing their parents.

ACTIVITY 2.1 – WATCH

Watch this video that explains intrinsic and extrinsic motivation and answer the questions that follow.

▶ www.educate*plus*.ie/go/intrinsic-extrinsic-motivation

1. What is the main difference between an intrinsic and an extrinsic reward?
2. How can we get our brains to motivate us to do the things worth doing?

ACTIVITY 2.2 – DISCUSS

A. In pairs, discuss and indicate whether each of the following actions are intrinsically motivated, extrinsically motivated or both. Give a reason for your answer.

	Action	Intrinsic	Extrinsic	Both	Reason
1	Participating in a sport because it's fun and you enjoy it.	○	○	○	
2	Spending time with someone to improve your popularity.	○	○	○	
3	Exercising because you enjoy physically challenging your body.	○	○	○	
4	Volunteering because it makes you feel good about yourself, and you enjoy when others compliment you for giving up your weekends to volunteer.	○	○	○	
5	Posting on TikTok to get likes and increase your views.	○	○	○	
6	Going for a run to increase your chances of winning a competition.	○	○	○	
7	Painting so that you can sell your art to make money.	○	○	○	
8	Going for a run because you find it relaxing or are trying to beat a personal record.	○	○	○	
9	Posting on Instagram to share your holiday with friends and get likes and positive comments.	○	○	○	
10	Spending time with someone because you enjoy their company.	○	○	○	
11	Cleaning your room to avoid making your parents angry.	○	○	○	
12	Exercising because you want to lose weight or fit into an outfit.	○	○	○	
13	Studying for your Geography exam because you enjoy learning about sustainability, but you also want to get good grades so that your mum will be proud of you.	○	○	○	

B. Reflection questions:

1. Which form of motivation do you think works best in the long term? Why?
2. Why do both forms of motivation overlap?
3. Thinking back to the video of Cristiano Ronaldo from the previous chapter (page 5), would you say he is intrinsically motivated, extrinsically motivated or both? Why?
4. Can you think of a time when you stayed motivated for a long time to achieve a goal? Were you intrinsically motivated, extrinsically motivated or both?

Intrinsic or extrinsic motivation: Which is best?

Intrinsic motivation

Intrinsic motivation, driven by personal enjoyment and passion, has been found to be more long-lasting. It empowers people to overcome challenges, explore their passions and achieve meaningful success, as they are doing it for personal pleasure and not for outward approval.

Extrinsic motivation

Extrinsic motivation, based on external rewards, can provide a short-term boost but may lead to burnout and a loss of inner drive in the long term. Also, when people rely too much on external motivation, they begin to compare themselves to others and may give too much weight to other people's opinions.

Having strong intrinsic motivation is much more important than relying solely on extrinsic motivation. Studies have found that in the long run, extrinsic motivation only truly works when you already have a genuine inner drive.

ACTIVITY 2.3 – READ

Read these two case studies and answer the questions that follow.

Case study 1

Anita is a passionate boxer who dedicates hours each week to practising and developing her skills. She genuinely loves sparring and finds joy in the process of improving her speed, endurance and balance. Anita sets personal goals for herself because she loves to feel like she is improving her game. Although Anita also likes competing and winning, she is more motivated by how she feels inside when she achieves new milestones.

1. Which form of motivation does Anita focus more heavily on? If you were to put a percentage on it, what would it be?
2. Do you think that Anita will stick with her personal goals in the long term? Why?
3. How do you think Anita's motivational approach supports her mental health and wellbeing?

Case study 2

Lily regularly uses fake tan, wears a lot of makeup, applies fake eyelashes and relies on filters when posting pictures online. Lily's main drive behind these choices is the desire to receive **external validation** (approval or recognition from others to feel worthy or confident) and to be seen as attractive by others. Lily's self-worth is heavily reliant on the amount of likes and positive feedback she receives online. She invests a large amount of time in preparing and capturing the perfect picture before posting it.

1. Which form of motivation does Lily focus more heavily on? If you were to put a percentage on it, what would it be?
2. What impact might this form of motivation have on Lily's emotional wellbeing?
3. How could Lily find a better balance between the two forms of motivation? What advice would you give her if you were her friend?

ACTIVITY 2.4 – THINK

Your teacher will designate one end of the classroom as 'Extrinsic Motivation' and the other end as 'Intrinsic Motivation'. They will then read out a scenario. After hearing the scenario, place yourself beside the type of motivation you think it reflects. Once you have taken your position, your teacher will add to the scenario by reading out several statements. After hearing each statement, move along the classroom to show where you think the person in the scenario falls on the scale of extrinsic to intrinsic motivation.

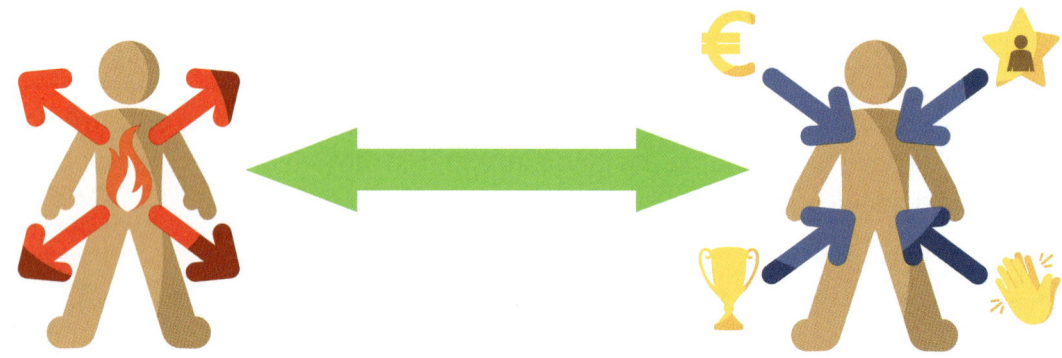

ACTIVITY 2.5 – THINK

Reflect on how intrinsic and extrinsic motivation play a role in your life by answering these questions:

1. Are you mainly driven by external rewards and recognition, or by internal motivation?
2. How does this impact your overall satisfaction and wellbeing?
3. What activities do you engage in simply because you enjoy them?
4. How can you become more intrinsically motivated in life?

Name one important thing you learned about intrinsic and extrinsic motivation in this chapter.

Related Learning Outcomes: 1.2, 1.7, 1.8.

CHAPTER 3

Understanding Personality Types

In this chapter we will:
- ✓ learn about the two main social personality types
- ✓ explore the introvert–extrovert spectrum and decide our position along this spectrum
- ✓ consider effective ways to show respect and offer support to individuals who have different personality types from our own.

KEY TERMS
Personality types
Introverts
Extroverts
Ambivert

 Have you ever thought about what your type of personality is?

Introverts and extroverts

While we are all unique and have our own distinct personalities, similar personality traits can be grouped together into different **personality types**. There are a number of different personality types, but many of them can be categorised under two main social types: introverts and extroverts. Understanding the differences between them can help us to navigate relationships better.

Introverts prefer spending time alone and enjoy quieter, more intimate settings. They gain energy from their inner world of thoughts and ideas, and tend to:
- be great listeners
- be observant
- have deep connections with a few close friends.

Introverts may feel drained in large social gatherings and need time alone to recharge.

Extroverts thrive in social situations and gain energy from being around others. They tend to:
- be outgoing
- be expressive
- enjoy being the centre of attention.

Extroverts love group activities and making new friends, and they often have a wide network of friends and acquaintances. They may find being alone challenging.

13

An **ambivert** is a person who has features of both an introvert and an extrovert, falling somewhere in between the two. They can switch between being more introverted or extroverted depending on their mood, the situation they're in and what they want to achieve. Ambiverts have the ability to adapt and feel comfortable in different social settings. They might enjoy spending time alone to recharge, but also thrive in social interactions and enjoy being around others.

Facts about introverts and extroverts

Being introverted or extroverted is influenced by our DNA.

Pretending to be extroverted when you're an introvert can negatively affect performance.

People who spend more than two hours a day on social media are often perceived by themselves and others as more outgoing and extroverted.

Introverts don't lack self-esteem. They accept themselves for who they are and expect others to do the same.

Extroverts tend to prefer immediate rewards and are more likely to engage in risk-taking behaviours, including extreme sports. They are sensitive to impulsive, reward-driven actions.

ACTIVITY 3.1 – WATCH

A. Watch this video about introverts and extroverts.

▶ www.educate*plus*.ie/go/introvert-vs-extrovert

B. Create one test question to assess someone's knowledge on any aspect of the video. In pairs, ask each other your test questions.

The introvert–extrovert spectrum

The introvert–extrovert spectrum is an imaginary line that shows different levels of being introverted or extroverted. The spectrum helps us understand that people can fall anywhere along the line, from being really introverted to really extroverted, or somewhere in between (an ambivert). We all have different preferences, needs and limits when it comes to socialising and recharging.

Introvert ⟵ **Ambivert** ⟶ **Extrovert**

Signs that you may be an introvert:	Signs that you may be an ambivert:	Signs that you may be an extrovert:
• You prefer solitude over company. • You prefer intimate gatherings over large ones. • You feel drained after being around a lot of people. • You can be overstimulated by external disturbances such as crowds, noise and chaotic environments. • You prefer to work alone rather than with a team. • You retreat inside your own mind. • You are self-reflective.	• Neither 'introvert' nor 'extrovert' feel accurate to describe your personality type. • You need alone time just as much as social time. • You prefer a balance of both solo and group work. • Too much alone time and too much time with others can feel draining. • You appreciate good conversation but also value comfortable silence. • Small talk doesn't bother you, though you also love deep conversations. • You have a lot of friends and a handful of close friends.	• Large events and groups of people excite you. • You feel drained spending too much time alone. • You enjoy collaborating and working with a team. • You're communicative and expressive. • You tend to focus on external things and seek connection. • You have varied friends, interests and hobbies.

ACTIVITY 3.2 – DISCUSS

A. In groups, draw a version of the introvert–extrovert spectrum on a piece of paper. Label 'Introvert' on one end, 'Extrovert' on the other and 'Ambivert' in the middle.

B. Discuss which of the following activities you prefer to do alone, with the company of others, or as a mix between the two, and why. Write your name and each activity where it best fits on the spectrum.
- Exercising
- Studying
- Solving problems
- Being comforted
- Cooking/baking
- Travelling
- Eating meals
- Watching movies or series
- Gaming
- Dining out

C. **Reflection questions:**
1. Is your group more introverted, extroverted or ambivert?
2. Did you learn anything surprising about your group during this activity?
3. Do you think that it's easier to be an introvert or extrovert in life? Why?

Relationships with people who have different personality types

Whether it's a friendship or a romantic relationship, introverted and extroverted people can make a great match. These two personality types often complement each other in social situations. Here are some points to consider about introvert-extrovert relationships:

- Introverts are typically quieter and tend to be listeners more than talkers. They also enjoy deeper one-on-one connections. Meanwhile, extroverts are more outgoing and social, and enjoy interacting in group settings. These differences can create a balanced dynamic in a relationship.
- Introverts may require more alone time to recharge their energy, while extroverts may seek more social interaction. Recognising and accommodating these differences without judgement is essential for maintaining a healthy balance.
- Open and honest communication is crucial in any relationship. Introverted and extroverted partners should express their needs, preferences and concerns to each other to ensure that each person understands the other.

ACTIVITY 3.3 – DISCUSS

As a class, brainstorm different situations in which introverts and extroverts may feel uncomfortable or misunderstood. For example, an introvert may feel uncomfortable at a large social gathering. Offer suggestions for how people with these personality types could handle the situations.

ACTIVITY 3.4 – READ

These three scenarios outline instances where extroverts and introverts have to work together. In groups, read the scenario that has been assigned to you. Discuss and propose strategies to accommodate both personality types in the scenario, ensuring that the strengths and needs of each person are considered. Each group will then present their ideas to the class.

Scenario 1: Working on a group presentation

Description: An extroverted student and an introverted student are assigned to work together on a group presentation for a CBA.

Challenge: Combining the extroverted student's enthusiasm for public speaking and collaboration with the introverted student's preference for thoughtful preparation and reflection.

Discussion points: How can they allocate tasks that play to each person's strengths? How can they create an inclusive presentation that allows the introverted student to contribute comfortably and confidently?

CHAPTER 3 – UNDERSTANDING PERSONALITY TYPES

Scenario 2: Planning a birthday celebration

Description: An extroverted friend and an introverted friend want to plan their joint sixteenth birthday celebrations.

Challenge: Balancing the extroverted friend's desire for social activities with the introverted friend's need for downtime and relaxation.

Discussion points: How can they create an itinerary that includes both social outings and quiet, relaxing moments? How can they ensure that the introverted friend's boundaries and preferences for alone time are respected, while still enjoying shared experiences?

Scenario 3: Starting an LGBTQI+ awareness campaign

Description: An extroverted student and an introverted student want to collaborate on the launch of an awareness campaign for LGBTQI+ rights.

Challenge: Combining the extroverted student's enthusiasm for public engagement and networking with the introverted student's attention to research and thoughtful messaging.

Discussion points: How can they use the extroverted student's social influence, while also ensuring that the introverted student's contributions are valued?

? How has your understanding of extroverts and introverts evolved throughout this chapter? Has it challenged any assumptions or stereotypes you might have had?

17

Related Learning Outcomes: 1.4, 1.6, 1.7, 1.8.

CHAPTER 4

Bias, Inequality and Exclusion

In this chapter we will:
- discuss the meanings of and connection between bias, inequality and exclusion
- identify the difference between exclusion and discrimination
- consider our own personal biases in life
- learn about how some people are more privileged in life than others.

KEY TERMS
Bias
Inequality
Exclusion
Discrimination
Privilege

? In your own words, describe what an equal and inclusive environment looks and feels like.

Understanding bias, inequality and exclusion

Equality, equity and inclusivity create positive relationships and environments. However, bias, inequality and exclusion can do the opposite:

Bias occurs when people perceive or assume things to be a certain way, even if it may not be accurate. We display bias when we make assumptions or judgements based on our personal experiences or beliefs.

Example: A student learns that their classmate is gay and begins making assumptions or judgements about their personality or interests based solely on their sexual orientation.

Inequality occurs when some people have more resources, chances to succeed and advantages in life than others.

Example: A student from a wealthy family can afford private tutoring sessions on a weekly basis to improve their Maths results, while their classmates can only afford tutoring once a month, or not at all.

Exclusion occurs when people are purposely left out or not allowed to take part in an activity. When someone is excluded, this means that a person or group will deliberately choose not to include them in something, or make them feel like they don't belong. Exclusion can have an impact on our self-worth and sense of connection and acceptance.

Example: A group of friends set up a group chat and intentionally leave out one or two friends.

18

It's important to note that discrimination goes a step further than exclusion. **Discrimination** occurs when someone treats another person unfairly or unequally based on who they are or what they believe. From a legal perspective, the Equal Status Act in Irish law prohibits discrimination on nine different grounds:

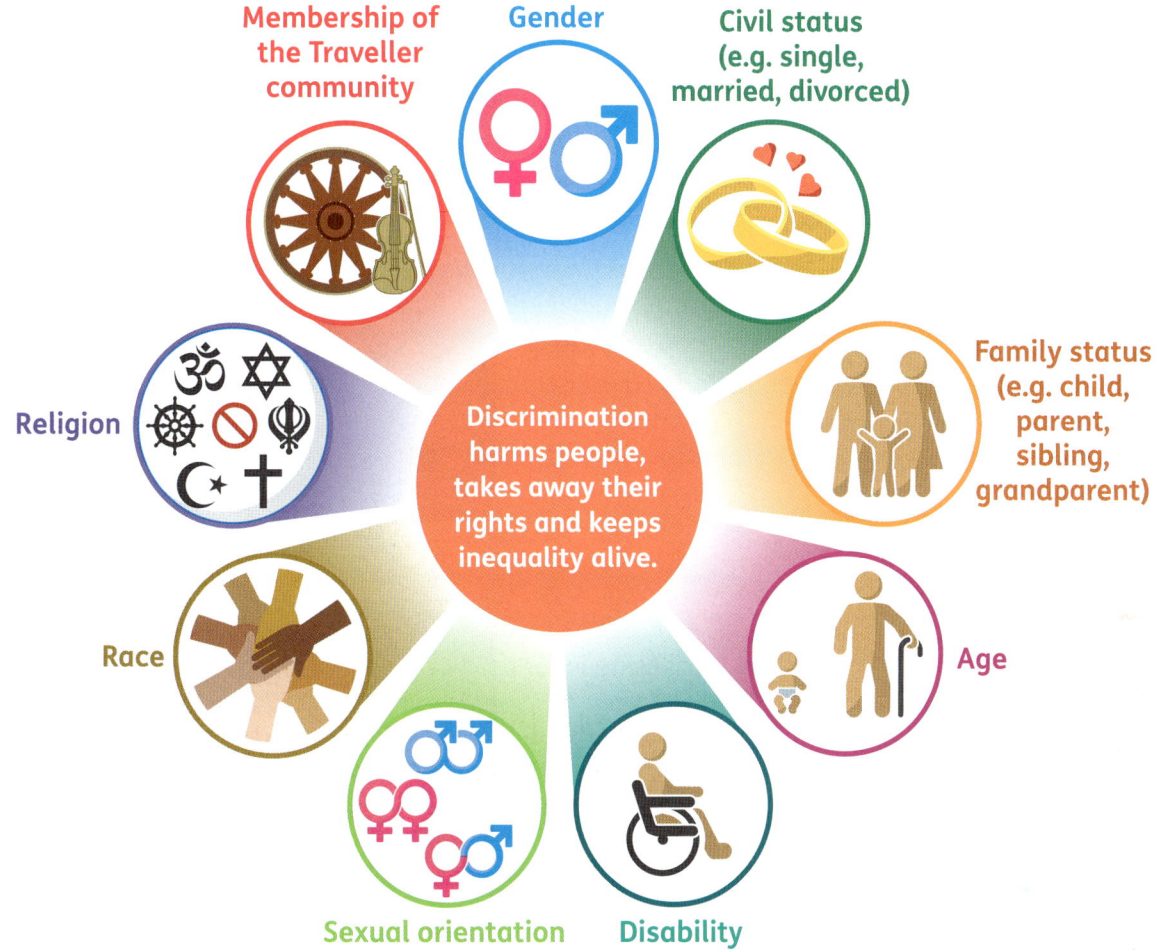

ACTIVITY 4.1 – READ

In groups, read the scenario below that has been assigned to you. Identify whether there is bias, inequality or exclusion present in the scenario, and discuss how it affects the person's life.

Scenario 1
Jasmine, a highly qualified woman, applies for a management position at a large company. Despite her expertise, she is passed over for the role in favour of a less-experienced male candidate.

Scenario 2
Raj, a man who has immigrated to a new country, applies for various job positions but receives very few interview callbacks. Frustrated, he decides to create an identical CV but changes his name to a more common local name. Surprisingly, he receives a higher number of interview invitations.

Scenario 3
Maria, a student from a low-income area, attends a school with limited resources and outdated facilities. The school struggles to provide quality education, which leaves Maria with fewer opportunities than the students attending well-funded private schools in wealthier areas.

Scenario 4
Alex, a student who has a learning disability, experiences ongoing difficulties in school. His class is large, and despite his teacher's efforts to assist him, he feels like he is not keeping up with his peers and is falling behind.

Scenario 5
Chris, who openly identifies as gay, senses he is being ignored by his classmates. Additionally, some of his peers make disrespectful remarks and deliberately exclude him from social activities.

Scenario 6
Sanah, a young Muslim woman, experiences discrimination when trying to rent an apartment. Despite her having a steady job and good references, landlords deny her applications based on her religious clothing.

Do we all experience bias?

Bias is a natural part of being human. It's our brain's way of simplifying information and making quick judgements. However, biases can unconsciously shape how we see and treat others, and sometimes lead to unfairness and discrimination. By acknowledging our biases and exploring their origins, we empower ourselves to:

- make more conscious choices
- challenge stereotypes (preconceived beliefs about people)
- treat everyone with respect and fairness.

ACTIVITY 4.2 – THINK

A. Individually, take this bias awareness survey to reflect on your own biases. Indicate whether you agree with, are unsure of or disagree with each statement. This activity can also be completed anonymously on the *You've Got This!* app.

	Statement	Agree	Unsure	Disagree
1	People who are more attractive have an easier time in life.	○	○	○
2	People who play video games are less academic.	○	○	○
3	People who are overweight are less disciplined with their health.	○	○	○
4	People who follow a vegan lifestyle are more compassionate towards animals and the environment.	○	○	○
5	People who enjoy reading are more intelligent than those who don't.	○	○	○
6	Boys are naturally better at sports than girls.	○	○	○
7	People who are introverted are less confident in social situations.	○	○	○
8	People who are part of the LGBTQI+ community are very vocal and opinionated.	○	○	○
9	People who don't wear makeup or dress nicely don't care about their appearance.	○	○	○
10	People with tattoos and piercings are less trustworthy.	○	○	○
11	People who listen to aggressive music are aggressive people.	○	○	○
12	People who don't use social media frequently are missing out on important social connections and opportunities.	○	○	○
13	Older people don't understand what it's like to be a teenager.	○	○	○
14	People who come from a lower-income background are less hardworking than those from higher-income backgrounds.	○	○	○

B. Calculate your overall score for the survey:

0 points for each 'Agree' response	
1 point for each 'Unsure' response	
2 points for each 'Disagree' response	
Total score	

C. Compare your score to the chart below to get your result.

24–28 points	Great job! You have demonstrated a strong awareness of bias.
20–23 points	Well done! You have some awareness of bias but could further explore certain areas.
10–19 points	There is room for improvement. Reflect on the statements and consider how bias may influence your perspectives.
0–9 points	Perhaps you could see this as an opportunity to learn more about bias.

Privilege

Privilege refers to advantages and opportunities that certain individuals enjoy due to factors such as race, gender and socio-economic status (where someone stands in terms of money, education and work). The unequal distribution of privilege leaves some people with greater access to resources, opportunities and social power. Examples of privilege include having:

- access to a safe, secure home life
- disposable income in the family, which can be used for holidays or school trips
- access to Wi-Fi
- access to healthcare and education.

Understanding privilege allows us to challenge and break down inequality. By doing this, we can create a society where everyone has equal opportunities to thrive.

ACTIVITY 4.3 – DISCUSS

A. Your teacher will assign the roles below to a few students in the class. These students will then line up at the back of the classroom. Each chosen student needs to imagine being in the shoes of their assigned person. Your teacher will then read out a number of statements, and the students should take a step forward if they believe the statement applies to their assigned person.

Rihanna: A woman from a middle-income background, originally from Latvia.

Jamal: A man of Nigerian heritage from a lower-income background.

Maria: A college student of Polish descent, living in Ireland.

Aiden: A man from a high-income Irish family.

Priya: An Indian-Irish woman from a low-income family, living in Ireland.

Mohammed: An immigrant from a lower-income background, who follows the Islamic faith.

Sofia: A transgender woman from a well-off family with mixed racial heritage.

Tao: A Chinese immigrant from a family with undocumented parents (no visa to stay in Ireland), adapting to life in Ireland.

Maya: A bisexual woman of German descent from a middle-income background, now living in a remote part of Ireland.

Elijah: A man evicted from his rented property and seeking alternative accommodation to avoid homelessness.

Ava: A woman who inherited money from her wealthy parents.

Javier: A father of five, working in an unreliable, low-paying job and living in rural Ireland.

B. Reflection questions:

1. Reflect on the concept of privilege and its influence on our lives. In what ways have you personally benefited from certain privileges?
2. Consider the experiences of the imaginary people in this activity. How do you think their experiences might differ from yours?
3. How can we use an awareness of privilege to be more empathetic and understanding, and support those who face barriers due to their lack of privilege?

Are there any biases you recognise in yourself? How can you overcome them?

Related Learning Outcomes: 1.4, 1.6, 1.7.

CHAPTER 5

Diversity and Inclusion

In this chapter we will:
- explore the meaning and benefits of diversity
- celebrate the differences between us
- explain the importance of being inclusive.

KEY TERMS
Diversity
Extremist
Inclusion

❓ What are some of the differences between the people in your community? What are some of the similarities?

What is diversity?

Diversity refers to the variety and differences found among individuals or groups within a community, organisation or society. These differences can include:

- race
- ethnicity
- gender
- age
- religion
- cultural background
- sexual orientation
- perspectives
- abilities
- skills.

Embracing diversity involves recognising, respecting and valuing these differences. Doing so helps to create an inclusive environment and promote equal opportunities for everyone.

'We all should know that diversity makes for a rich tapestry, and we must understand that all the threads of the tapestry are equal in value no matter what their colour.' – *Maya Angelou*

23

ACTIVITY 5.1 – DISCUSS

In this activity, we are going to play Diversity Bingo.

A. You will be given a bingo card (like the example below) that contains different characteristics of diversity. Walk around the room and speak with other students in order to find someone who matches the description in each square. When you find a match, write that student's name or initials on the square. This student's name can only appear on your card once. When you have filled out a line vertically, horizontally or diagonally with names, you can call out 'bingo!' to win.

DIVERSITY BINGO

Find someone who ...

speaks more than three languages	was born in a different country	knows sign language	has never read a Harry Potter book
has lived on a farm	has won a table quiz	observes Ramadan	does Irish dancing
loves cycling	likes Mars bars	plays a musical instrument	has a library book
is an only child	visited another country last year	has a part-time job	is a vegetarian

B. Reflection questions:
1. What did you learn about the diversity within your class group?
2. How does respecting diversity benefit a community?
3. How can we celebrate diversity and promote inclusivity in our daily lives?

The benefits of diversity

Diversity has many benefits in society, workplaces, education and communities:

- People have different backgrounds, cultures and experiences. They also have a unique combination of interests, hobbies and talents. When we have diversity, we get to learn about and appreciate these differences, and learn from each other.

- Diverse teams consider multiple viewpoints, leading to better decision making and improved outcomes.

- Diversity brings different perspectives and experiences, leading to more creative solutions to problems.

- Interacting with diverse people expands knowledge, promotes personal growth and builds empathy.

- Diversity reduces discrimination and allows for a sense of belonging for all members of society.

- Promoting diversity helps to create a more just, fair and equitable society, where all individuals have equal opportunities and are not held back by discrimination or prejudice.

- Having diversity helps us to be more accepting and inclusive of others, and to treat everyone with kindness and respect regardless of what they look like or where they come from. This is important because it helps to create a better and more peaceful world.

ACTIVITY 5.2 – READ

In pairs, read the following diversity scenarios and suggest how they can be beneficial to you. The first one has been done as an example.

	Scenario	Benefit
1	Having a classmate whose skin colour is different from yours.	You can learn about their experiences and how they see the world, which can help you see things from a different perspective.
2	Having a friend who grew up in a different country from yours.	
3	Having a friend who is differently abled from you.	
4	Having a friend who has a different sexual orientation from yours.	
5	Having a friend from a different ethnic background from yours (e.g. a member of the Traveller community).	
6	Having a classmate who has a different set of religious beliefs or worldview from yours.	
7	Having a friend who sees things differently from you.	

Celebrating difference

We are all different and unique, and this is something to celebrate! Being interested in and open to the differences between us allows us to:

- open our minds to new ideas
- discover new perspectives
- experience different opportunities
- make new friends
- challenge stereotypes

It's also important to embrace our own cultures, backgrounds, interests and identities. We should be proud of who we are and celebrate our individuality.

ACTIVITY 5.3 – WATCH

In pairs, watch this video about celebrating cultural differences and answer the questions that follow.

▶ www.educate*plus*.ie/go/cultural-differences

1. What elements are part of a person's culture?
2. Give two reasons why it's important to embrace other people's cultures.
3. In your opinion, do you think that labelling people is appropriate?
4. What part of your culture are you most proud of?

ACTIVITY 5.4 – DISCUSS

> 'We are far more united and have far more in common with each other than things that divide us.' – *Jo Cox*

This quote is from a speech made by Jo Cox, who was a Member of Parliament in the UK. In 2016, she was murdered by a far-right **extremist**, who is someone who holds extreme political, social or religious views.

Do you agree or disagree with the statement made by Jo? In pairs, discuss your thoughts on it. Think about the other people in your class and community. Try to give some examples of things you have in common, if you agree with the statement.

After you have discussed in pairs, share your thoughts with the class.

The importance of inclusion

Inclusion means being open to everyone and treating all people fairly and equally. It has significant benefits for individuals, communities and society as a whole:

> Inclusion embraces diversity in all its forms, whether it's related to race, ethnicity, gender, sexual orientation, disability or any other characteristic. It promotes a deeper understanding of various cultures, perspectives and life experiences.

> Inclusive environments make individuals feel accepted, valued and welcomed. When people feel like they belong, they are more likely to engage with and contribute positively to their communities. As well as that, feeling included and accepted is crucial for mental health and emotional wellbeing.

> Inclusive education and workplaces encourage collaboration and cooperation among people with different abilities and backgrounds. This creates a rich learning experience, where everyone can develop new skills and perspectives.

> Inclusion challenges stereotypes and prejudices by promoting positive interactions and relationships between people from diverse backgrounds. It helps break down barriers and reduce discrimination and bias. When people interact with others who have different life experiences, they develop empathy and compassion.

> Inclusion teaches people to put themselves in others' shoes. This can lead to more empathy and help to reduce conflicts.

ACTIVITY 5.5 – THINK

A. In groups, brainstorm your understanding of inclusion. Write words or sentences to express what your definition of it is.

B. Suggest ways that your school is inclusive for all students, and any other ways it can be more inclusive. For example: All students receive equal opportunities to participate in extracurricular activities.

ACTIVITY 5.6 – DISCUSS

In groups, read these descriptions of four mystery celebrities. See if you can guess who each person is based on their diverse backgrounds.

- I am a singer and an actor.
- My mum is Catholic, and my dad is Muslim.
- I am spiritual but not religious.
- I come from Kosovo.
- I have toured with Drake and Coldplay.
- I have been an *X Factor* judge and a voice coach on *The Voice*.

- I was a promising athlete before I was an actor.
- I was born in Maynooth, Co. Kildare.
- I attended Trinity College in Dublin.
- I am a big fan of Dermot Kennedy and Lorde.
- I can sing and play the piano.
- I support mental health charities.
- I was nominated for an Academy Award (Oscar).

- I am an American actor.
- I am Jewish.
- My father is of Russian-Jewish descent, and my mother is of Moroccan-Jewish descent.
- I star in the Netflix show *Stranger Things*.
- In 2023, I came out as gay in a video I posted to my TikTok account.

- I was born on 1 September 1996.
- I was a backup dancer for Selena Gomez before becoming a Disney star.
- I am an actor, singer and published author.
- My Academy Award (Oscar) look inspired a Barbie doll.
- My father is of African-American descent, and my mother has German and Scottish ancestry.
- I am known by a single name.

ACTIVITY 5.7 – CREATE

As a class, plan a 'Diversity Day' in your school to promote inclusivity and celebrate differences among students and staff. Here are some ideas for planning your Diversity Day:

- Organise a lunch where students and staff bring in dishes from different cultures.
- Organise a cultural fair where students and staff can set up stands representing different countries and cultures. These stands can showcase traditional clothing, food, music and dance from different countries.
- Organise art projects, poetry readings or storytelling sessions that highlight the beauty of different cultures and the importance of inclusivity.
- Set up language exchange sessions where students can teach each other basic phrases in different languages.
- Host a film screening of a movie that explores themes of diversity and inclusion, followed by a discussion session.

What do you think is the biggest benefit of a diverse and inclusive society?

Related Learning Outcomes: 1.3, 1.7, 4.4.

CHAPTER 6

Mistakes, Criticism and Self-Compassion

In this chapter we will:
- ✓ explore how to cope with mistakes
- ✓ investigate how to deal with criticism from ourselves and others
- ✓ discuss how we can use self-compassion when we make mistakes and self-criticise.

KEY TERMS
Criticism
Constructive
Destructive
Self-criticism
Self-compassion

? When was the last time you made a mistake? How did you react to it?

Coping with mistakes

Everyone makes mistakes, from your teachers to the biggest movie or sports stars. Mistakes are a natural aspect of life. It's important to recognise that mistakes are valuable opportunities for learning and growth.

Some mistakes are bigger than others, and they may or may not have a quick solution. Nevertheless, it's essential to accept our mistakes and focus on moving forward, rather than dwell on the past and self-blame.

To effectively cope with mistakes:

1. Separate yourself from the mistake
Remember that a mistake doesn't define your worth as a person. No one is perfect, and it's okay to make errors.

2. Take responsibility
Confront your mistakes head-on, take ownership of what happened and apologise if needed. Avoid making excuses.

29

3. Understand the mistake

If you're unsure about what went wrong, talk to others involved to gain a better understanding of the situation.

4. Seek solutions

Most mistakes have solutions, so think about how you can improve the situation. Always try to stay solution focused.

5. Talk about it

When dealing with significant mistakes, don't hesitate to talk to your friends or family about it. They may provide valuable insights and support.

6. Seek help if needed

If you find it challenging to accept your mistakes and move on, consider talking to someone you trust or seeking professional help.

7. Value the learning process

Recognise that mistakes are opportunities to gain knowledge. Viewing mistakes this way can help you develop and improve as a person. You will make mistakes in life, but how you handle and learn from them is what truly matters.

TIPS

Apologising effectively and sincerely is an important skill to learn. A sincere apology is not always easy to offer, but it can help you repair relationships and take responsibility for mistakes. Here are some basic tips on how to apologise effectively:

- Start your apology by saying, 'I'm sorry' to show that you acknowledge your mistake and are taking responsibility for it.
- Explain what you're sorry for. Instead of just saying, 'I'm sorry for everything', say, 'I'm sorry for what I said/did.' It's important to be specific.
- Show that you genuinely feel bad about your actions. You can say: 'I feel really upset that I have hurt you.'
- Don't make excuses or blame others. Instead, focus on your actions and their impact.
- Give the other person a chance to express their feelings.
- Let the person know that you will do your best to ensure that it does not happen again.
- If possible, offer to make things right or help fix the situation.
- Understand that the other person might need time to forgive you. Be patient and give them space.

CHAPTER 6 – MISTAKES, CRITICISM AND SELF-COMPASSION

ACTIVITY 6.1 – DISCUSS

In groups, read the scenario below that has been assigned to you. Discuss and identify what can be learned from the mistake.

Scenario 1
After getting a glass of orange juice, I didn't put the lid back on the bottle properly. When my mother shook the bottle, orange juice spilled all over the place.

Scenario 2
When I called over to my friend's house, I left my bike in the driveway, behind their car. My friend's dad reversed into it.

Scenario 3
I played video games after school, then decided to watch my favourite series. There wasn't enough time to study for the exam that I had the next day. I didn't do well in the exam.

Scenario 4
At school, I didn't like the lunch my mother packed for me, so I ate nothing. When I got home, I snapped at her because I was tired and hungry.

ACTIVITY 6.2 – THINK

In pairs, evaluate the mistakes below and identify ways to cope with them or correct them.

	Mistake	How to cope with it or correct it
1	I lost a book belonging to my teacher.	
2	I messed up the shot during a soccer game and it went wide.	practice shooting
3	I forgot to dress up for a charity day at my school.	set a reminder for next time
4	After class, my teacher told me I was talking too much.	be quiet next time and apologize
5	During Art class I accidentally broke another student's pottery vase.	Say sorry and offer your own
6	I gave the wrong answer in the table quiz, and we came second place.	say your sorry and learn more
7	While giving directions, I directed the person the wrong way.	learn how to give directions properly
8	I called someone a mean name when I was angry.	say sorry and apolgize

Coping with criticism

Criticism is any form of critical feedback, whether positive or negative, that assesses a person's character, skills or creative work. It has the potential to be:

- **Constructive**: Helpful and valuable, leading to growth. For example: Your teacher gives you detailed feedback on an assignment, including steps for improving your work.
- **Destructive**: Harmful, leading to feelings of inadequacy (feeling not good enough) and low self-esteem. For example: Someone tells you that you're really bad at dancing or singing and that you should never perform again.

Self-criticism is the act of judging yourself critically, often focusing on personal weaknesses, mistakes or areas for improvement. It involves evaluating your own actions and behaviour.

When faced with criticism, your initial reaction might be to either take the negative aspects to heart, or to completely dismiss the criticism. However, by having a balanced mindset, you can use both positive and negative criticism to enhance your self-esteem.

Here is some advice on coping with criticism from others:

Be open to learning from others
When someone provides constructive criticism, actively listen to understand what parts you agree or disagree with. Ask follow-up questions and engage with any feedback. Be open and willing to address and learn from your errors.

Consider the source
Think about who is giving you the criticism. Sometimes, your critics might offer you valuable insights that you can learn from. Don't dismiss criticism from genuine sources.

Discard destructive criticism
Truly destructive and toxic criticism creates a negative environment, which makes it very difficult for you to improve. Try to pick and choose what you take in and what you ignore. If toxic people offer you only attacks instead of constructive feedback, take a deep breath and move on to hear from more helpful sources.

Recognise the positives
When you receive criticism, it means that someone else recognised a way that you could improve. While you might not want someone else to see your mistakes, their constructive criticism could provide you with the steps necessary to become better than ever before.

Mind your mental health
Even if a person offers negative feedback in the most constructive way possible, it can still have a major impact on your mental health and self-confidence. Set boundaries and give yourself space from others when you need to.

Seek out constructive criticism
If you can find reliable people who'll always offer constructive criticism, make it a point to consider their points of view.

Realise your worth
Receiving feedback and hearing critical comments can be upsetting. Everyone, including highly successful people, can find it difficult to move past harsh criticisms. However, it's important to understand that criticism isn't an attack on you as a person. Learn to separate yourself from your mistakes. Realising your worth involves understanding your strengths and knowing how to address your weaknesses.

CHAPTER 6 – MISTAKES, CRITICISM AND SELF-COMPASSION

ACTIVITY 6.3 – READ

Read these four scenarios and answers the questions that follow.

Scenario 1: Art class feedback

You're in an Art class, and you've just finished a painting. Your classmate, Suzie, takes a look at your painting and wants to give you feedback. Suzie says, 'I really like your painting, but I think the colours are a bit dull. Have you considered using brighter shades?'

1. Is this an example of constructive or destructive criticism?
2. How might you best respond to this criticism?

Scenario 2: Comment about appearance

At school, someone makes a hurtful comment about your appearance. The person says, 'You look terrible in that outfit. You should never wear clothes like that – they don't suit you.'

1. Is this an example of constructive or destructive criticism?
2. How might you best respond to this criticism?

Scenario 3: School presentation feedback

After you have given a presentation to your class, your teacher, Mr Murphy, wants to provide you with feedback. Mr Murphy tells you, 'Your presentation was very informative, but it would be even better if you added some visuals to support your points. What do you think?'

1. Is this an example of constructive or destructive criticism?
2. How might you best respond to this criticism?

Scenario 4: Comment on social media

Someone leaves a hurtful comment on your social media post. The comment reads: 'You're so stupid. Your posts are a load of rubbish.'

1. Is this an example of constructive or destructive criticism?
2. How might you best respond to this criticism?

Using self-compassion

Self-compassion is an attitude that involves treating ourselves with warmth, kindness and understanding in challenging times. It recognises that suffering and personal failure are a part of the human experience, and it plays an important role in making mistakes and self-criticism:

Mistakes
When we make mistakes, we need to show self-compassion by being understanding towards ourselves. We should acknowledge and address our negative emotions in a balanced and healthy way – this means neither suppressing them nor letting them overwhelm us.

Self-criticism
Balancing self-criticism with self-compassion is crucial for a positive self-image and good emotional wellbeing. It can be healthy to be critical of ourselves in order to grow and learn. However, we should never be too hard on ourselves – this is very harmful to our emotional wellbeing and can be counterproductive.

Here are some ways that you can be more compassionate towards yourself:

- Be patient and kind to yourself. It's okay if you don't always get things right or see immediate results. Remember to forgive yourself and let go, as it's healthier in the long run.
- Try writing down the self-talk you have after a bad day and reflect on whether you would speak to a friend in the same way. Being mindful of negative thoughts can help you realise how hurtful they can be.
- Engage your senses to relax and destress. Enjoy the scent of candles or body lotion, listen to calming music, practise some mindfulness, or take breaks from digital screens and explore nature's beauty by walking or cycling.

ACTIVITY 6.4 – READ

In groups, read this case study and answer the questions that follow.

Case study

Emilia is 15. She is great at sports, is a good singer and does well at school. She is considered by everyone to be very ambitious and high achieving. Last week, she got her English exam results and was disappointed to see that she received a much lower mark than she expected. She started to feel upset and frustrated with herself.

1. What kind of thoughts and self-talk do you think Emilia might be experiencing?
2. Do you think Emilia's self-criticism is constructive?
3. How can Emilia practise self-compassion in this situation?
4. Can you suggest some self-compassionate statements Emilia could tell herself?
5. How might practising self-compassion affect Emilia's emotional wellbeing and future approach to challenges?

CHAPTER 6 – MISTAKES, CRITICISM AND SELF-COMPASSION

ACTIVITY 6.5 – CREATE

Practise self-compassion by keeping a self-compassion journal for a week. Write about how you respond to the following with self-compassion:

- daily experiences
- challenges
- mistakes.

Include moments of self-criticism and how you can turn those negative thoughts into self-compassionate ones. When the week is over, have a class discussion in which you share your experiences and insights.

Day	Daily experiences	Challenges	Mistakes	How I responded with self-compassion
Monday				
Tuesday				
Wednesday				
Thursday				
Friday				
Saturday				
Sunday				

? Identify one way that you can use self-compassion when you make a mistake or self-criticise.

Related Learning Outcomes: 1.3, 1.8.

CHAPTER 7

Kindness

In this chapter we will:
- ✓ discuss the meaning, science and benefits of kindness
- ✓ explore self-kindness and evaluate how kind we are to ourselves
- ✓ examine how to nurture self-kindness in our everyday lives.

KEY TERMS
Kindness
Self-kindness

❓ What is kindness? As a class, brainstorm a list of kind acts in order to gain an understanding of the term.

What is kindness?

Kindness is the quality or act of being generous, helpful and caring towards others. It can mean different things to different people, and some examples include:

- saying kind words
- performing kind deeds
- showing kind attitudes towards others.

Kindness plays an important role in our wellbeing. Research has shown that kindness improves our physical and emotional health, regardless of whether we are being kind to others, receiving kindness or witnessing kindness.

The science of kindness

Kindness can help us feel happier

Studies show that acts of kindness trigger the release of the hormone dopamine in our brains, leading to an improved mood. This is commonly known as the 'helper's high'.

Kindness is good for the heart

Acts of kindness often make us feel good inside, triggering the release of the hormone oxytocin in the body. Oxytocin, in turn, causes the release of nitric oxide, a chemical that widens our blood vessels, lowers our blood pressure and protects our heart.

CHAPTER 7 – KINDNESS

Kindness helps slow ageing
Scientific studies have found that kindness can have an impact on the ageing process. Practising kindness helps boost levels of a chemical associated with happiness and relaxation. This chemical reduces levels of molecules linked to ageing in the body.

Kindness improves relationships
We usually like people who show us kindness. This is because kindness decreases the emotional distance between people and makes us feel more connected. Being kind to each other helps us to strengthen our existing relationships and to create new ones.

Kindness is contagious
When we are kind, we inspire others to be kind. Studies show that kindness actually creates a ripple effect that spreads outwards to other people. This means that when you are kind to one person, your act of kindness may positively affect many others.

ACTIVITY 7.1 – WATCH

A. Watch this Christmas advertisement titled 'Give a Little Love' and answer the questions that follow.

▶ www.educate*plus*.ie/go/give-little-love

1. What is the key message of the advertisement?
2. The John Lewis Christmas advertisements are quite popular. Based on what you have seen, why do you think this is?
3. Describe a time when you have been kind to someone else, or they have been kind to you. How did it make you feel?
4. Write an alternative title for the advertisement.

B. Design a poster that encourages others to be kind and #GiveALittleLove.

C. Research another John Lewis Christmas advertisement where kindness is a central theme.

Self-kindness

Just as you show kindness and compassion to others, you must also show kindness towards yourself. **Self-kindness** involves:

- treating yourself with compassion, understanding and gentleness
- being caring and nurturing towards yourself, especially during times of difficulty or failure, or when facing personal challenges
- acknowledging and accepting your imperfections, mistakes and limitations without self-criticism or self-judgement
- being understanding and patient with yourself, recognising that everyone is human.

Self-kindness is not about self-indulgence or avoiding growth and improvement. It's about providing yourself with emotional support, reassurance and motivation in a positive and caring manner.

By cultivating self-kindness, you can develop a healthier relationship with yourself, leading to increased self-esteem, reduced stress and improved overall wellbeing. It's an essential component of self-care and self-compassion, and can allow you to have a more positive outlook on life.

ACTIVITY 7.2 – THINK

A. How kind are you to yourself? Take this quiz to find out. This activity can also be completed on the *You've Got This!* app.

Instructions: Rate each statement below on a scale of 1 to 5, with 1 indicating 'Not at all' and 5 indicating 'Absolutely'. Be honest with yourself, and remember that there are no right or wrong answers.

	Statement	1	2	3	4	5
1	When I make a mistake, I don't criticise or blame myself.					
2	When I compare myself to others, I don't feel inadequate or that I don't measure up.					
3	I am understanding and patient with myself when facing challenges or setbacks.					
4	I find it easy to forgive myself for past mistakes or regrets.					
5	I take time to engage in activities that make me feel happy and fulfilled.					
6	I tend to focus on my strengths rather than my flaws and weaknesses.					
7	I treat myself with the same kindness and compassion that I show to my friends.					
8	I am open and honest with myself about my feelings and needs.					
9	I believe that making mistakes is a normal part of learning and growing.					
10	I practise self-care regularly and prioritise my wellbeing.					
11	I am accepting of myself, including my unique qualities and differences from others.					
12	I feel comfortable seeking help and support from others when needed.					
13	I don't tend to dwell on negative thoughts and experiences.					
14	I acknowledge and celebrate my achievements and successes.					
15	I am aware of the impact of my self-talk and try to make it more positive.					

B. Add up your total score and compare it to the chart below for your results.

15–30	**Low self-kindness:** You might be too hard on yourself. Try to practise more self-compassion and acknowledge your worth.
31–45	**Moderate self-kindness:** You have room for improvement. Be more mindful of how you treat yourself and work on developing self-kindness habits.
46–75	**High self-kindness:** You are doing well in treating yourself with kindness. Keep practising self-kindness and continue to prioritise your wellbeing.
	Remember, this quiz is just a starting point for self-reflection. Focus on areas that need improvement and try to nurture self-kindness in your daily life.

CHAPTER 7 – KINDNESS

How to nurture self-kindness

Self-kindness

Have a good night's sleep
Teenagers need between eight and ten hours of sleep a night. When you have a good night's sleep, your body can repair itself and get you ready for the next day. It also makes you feel less irritable.

Use kindness meditation
By meditating, you reduce your stress levels and create a more positive headspace. Meditating encourages your body and brain to fully relax, meaning you can think more clearly.

Practise gratitude
Practising gratitude means taking time to reflect on the things you're grateful for, whether it's a kind friend or a great day at school. Being thankful helps you to become a more positive person, who can show more compassion.

Exercise
Exercise is a great stress reducer. When you exercise, your brain releases mood-boosting brain chemicals such as endorphins and dopamine, which help you feel happier.

Believe in yourself
It's important to know you can achieve your dreams and the things you work hard for.

Be patient
No one is good at everything straight away. If you're struggling with something, try to think of the word 'yet': 'I'm not good at Spanish yet.' With that one little word, you can change your mindset and achieve whatever goals you have.

Ask for help
It can sometimes be difficult to ask for help, especially if it's for something you feel you should be good at or be able to do alone. However, we all need support from time to time. Asking for help when you need it will make you feel better, and the other person will feel better knowing they've done something kind for you.

Do something you love
Ensure that, at least once a day, you set some time aside to do something you love. It could be reading, watching TV or playing a sport. It's very important to feel happy and relaxed.

Practise speaking positively
Changing the way you think and talk to yourself can make a big difference in how you feel. For example, rather than saying, 'I failed, and I'm embarrassed', try reframing it positively by saying, 'I gave my best effort, and I was courageous.' Speaking kindly to yourself can help you feel calm, happy and more positive.

Note down what you love about yourself
Making a list of the things you like about yourself can help you feel happier. It might be that you have lovely eyes, that you're a good friend or that you are a fast swimmer. Whatever it is, write it down and read it from time to time to remind yourself.

ACTIVITY 7.3 – READ

In groups, read this case study and answer the questions that follow.

Case study

Emma is 15 years old and is doing her Junior Cycle. She is very bright and ambitious, and is actively involved in extracurricular activities such as sports and choir. Despite her achievements, Emma struggles with high levels of self-criticism and tends to set unrealistic standards for herself. She often feels overwhelmed by exam pressures and social expectations, which leads to frequent feelings of anxiety and self-doubt.

Over the past few weeks, her family has noticed that she hasn't been herself. She has become disinterested in her work. She often expresses that she doesn't feel good enough, and she has started to isolate herself from her friends. Her family is concerned about her emotional wellbeing and the impact it may have on her exam results and overall happiness.

1. Despite her achievements, what are some challenges that Emma faces in her academic and personal life?
2. How has Emma's behaviour changed over the past few weeks, and what are some specific concerns her family has regarding her emotional wellbeing?
3. How might Emma's family and friends support her during this challenging time?
4. What steps could Emma take to address her emotional wellbeing and help her manage exam pressures effectively?
5. How can Emma be kinder to herself? Suggest three ways.
6. How can Emma reframe her self-talk to be more positive? What can she say to herself?

ACTIVITY 7.4 – THINK

We are going to do some self-kindness meditation in this activity. Find a comfortable and quiet space in the classroom. Close your eyes and take a few deep breaths. Relax and reflect on the questions below as they are asked by your teacher.

1. How do you feel about yourself on a daily basis?
2. Are there times when you are too hard on yourself? If so, why?
3. What self-kindness practices do you think could benefit you?
4. Think about a moment when you were kind to yourself during a challenging time. How did showing kindness to yourself help you navigate the difficult situation?
5. List three things you appreciate about yourself and why.

> **?** What three things will you work on from the 'How to nurture self-kindness' list between now and the summer holidays?

Related Learning Outcomes: 1.3, 4.1.

CHAPTER 8

The Science of Happiness

In this chapter we will:
- explore the science of happiness
- identify ways to improve our happiness journey
- recognise things we are grateful for.

KEY TERMS
Happiness
Science of happiness
Flourishing

? Identify three things in your life that make you happy. Why do you think these things make you happy?

What is happiness?

Happiness is a state of emotional wellbeing that encompasses:
- positive emotions
- contentment
- a sense of fulfilment.

It can be experienced in small everyday moments of joy or during significant life achievements and the journey towards them. Happiness is unique to each person, and the things that bring happiness can vary widely. People may feel happiness when they:
- spend time with loved ones
- pursue passions
- accomplish goals
- connect with nature
- practise simple acts of kindness and gratitude.

The beauty of happiness lies in its ability to evolve and adapt to the ever-changing landscape of our lives.

What is the science of happiness?

The **science of happiness**, or positive psychology, studies wellbeing and how to achieve happiness, life satisfaction and positive emotions in both individuals and communities. It explores the factors that contribute to humans **flourishing**, which involves not just the absence of negative emotions but also the presence of positive ones.

41

Is happiness a journey or a destination?

'Happiness is a journey, not a destination' is a popular saying. It suggests that humans shouldn't believe that reaching a certain life goal, such as finding a great job or meeting the perfect partner, will reward them with happiness. Instead, it's the journey to these goals and how we live our lives that bring happiness. But is this really true? Let's investigate this using the science of happiness:

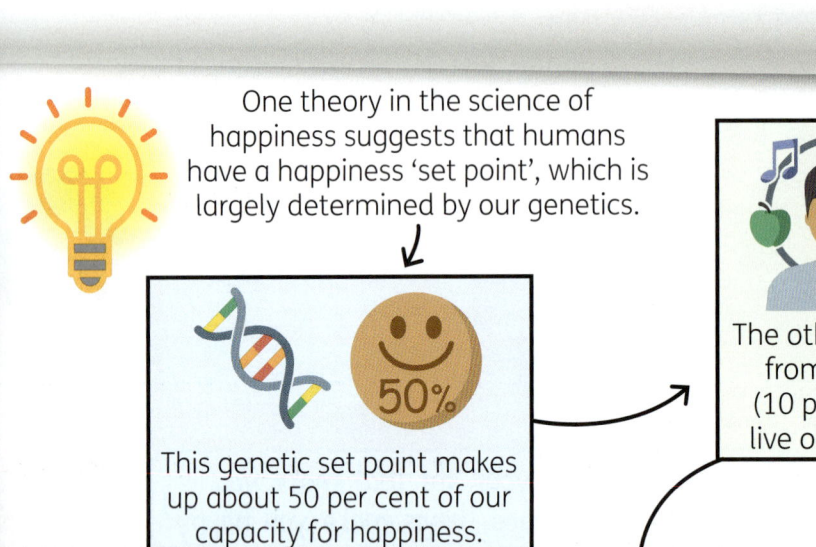

One theory in the science of happiness suggests that humans have a happiness 'set point', which is largely determined by our genetics.

This genetic set point makes up about 50 per cent of our capacity for happiness.

The other 50 per cent comes from our circumstances (10 per cent) and how we live our lives (40 per cent).

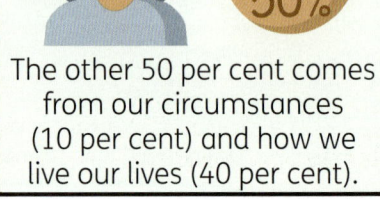

Our overall wellbeing is significantly influenced by our set point, which varies from person to person. Therefore, people with higher set points tend to experience greater happiness most of the time compared to those with lower set points, who naturally experience a less joyful outlook.

As we go through life, we swing back and forth around this set point. Unhappy life events can temporarily lower our happiness levels below the set point, while positive and exciting events can temporarily increase our happiness levels above it.

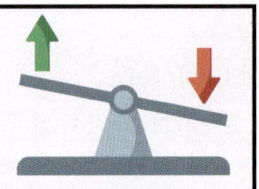

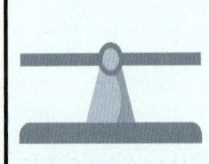

Over time, once the effects of these events normalise or change, our happiness levels tend to return to the original set point. For instance, we might experience the 'holiday blues' after returning from a holiday – our happiness levels go from high to low as we get back into our everyday routines, before returning to the set point.

Likewise, once you arrive at a destination in your life that brings you happiness, the feeling may not last. For example, after getting what you think is your dream job, you might discover that it brings you a lot of negative stress due to the additional workload.

Conclusion:
According to the theory outlined above, there is a lot of truth in the saying 'Happiness is a journey, not a destination.' If you do reach one of your life goals, you may indeed feel happier, but only temporarily. It's our genetic set point, the journey to these goals and how we live our lives that really influence how happy we are. We will all experience events in life that will affect our levels of happiness, both positively and negatively, and this is a normal part of living.

CHAPTER 8 – THE SCIENCE OF HAPPINESS

ACTIVITY 8.1 – THINK

A. In groups, think about what happiness is. What does it look like, sound like and feel like? Note down your thoughts. Some examples are given below.

Happiness		
Looks like	Sounds like	Feels like
Bright eyes	Laughter	Gratefulness
food / food *cluichí ar líne / videogames*	*music / ceol*	

B. Reflection questions:
1. After hearing from your classmates, do you think that there is one definition of happiness?
2. Should we expect to always be happy? Why?

C. Music often brings happiness. As a class, brainstorm songs that make you happy and choose a song to play at the end of this lesson.

ACTIVITY 8.2 – WATCH

Watch this video that outlines habits that may bring you happiness in your life and answer the questions that follow.

▶ www.educate*plus*.ie/go/happiness-habits

1. List ten habits that we can develop to become happier.
2. Which of these ten habits do you feel you could add to your life to support your level of happiness? Why?
3. How can you incorporate them into your daily life?

Improving your happiness journey

Your day-to-day life activity is responsible for a significant amount of your happiness. Regardless of your genetic set point and circumstances outside of your control, you can choose to incorporate activities into your life that will improve your happiness journey and general wellbeing. Here are four activities that you can do straight away:

1. Be kind

Research shows that we have the ability to become happier by engaging in acts of kindness towards others. The more compassionate you are, the happier your life journey appears to be. A study found that students who performed five weekly acts of kindness over six weeks experienced a significant increase in their happiness levels compared to a control group.

2. Practise gratitude

Practising gratitude can significantly contribute to our overall sense of happiness. It's one of the easiest life adjustments to make, as it requires very little effort. Studies have found that:
- people who practise gratitude tend to find joy in the simple pleasures that are accessible to most individuals
- keeping a daily or weekly gratitude journal can make finding happiness easier.

'In daily life we must see that it is not happiness that makes us grateful, but gratefulness that makes us happy.' – Brother David Steindl-Rast

3. Meditate

Regular meditation practice has the power to rewire your brain so that you can become happier. Starting your day with just five to ten minutes of meditation will help you to develop your happiness. Numerous studies have shown that meditation can:
- boost happiness levels by reducing stress hormones
- reduce anxiety
- stop rumination (thinking over things repeatedly).

4. Build quality relationships

If happiness is a journey and not a destination, then the people who accompany you on this journey can significantly impact your wellbeing. Developing and nurturing meaningful relationships is a key factor in finding and maintaining happiness. A 75-year study found that those who experienced the highest levels of joy were the ones who had strong and meaningful social connections.

ACTIVITY 8.3 – CREATE

A. What is gratitude? What does it mean to be grateful?

B. Watch this video that outlines the things that Oprah Winfrey is grateful for. Individually, write down five things that you are grateful for in your own life.

▶ www.educate*plus*.ie/go/oprah-winfrey

C. As a class, create a gratitude jar. Think of one thing that you are most grateful for today and write it down on a slip of paper. Then place the paper in the gratitude jar. Continue adding more things to the jar in future classes.

Date:
Today I'm grateful for:
My dog

Date:
Today I'm grateful for:
My best friend

Gratitude Jar

CHAPTER 8 – THE SCIENCE OF HAPPINESS

Here are some tips for choosing happiness:
- Don't be afraid of change.
- Laugh often.
- Allow yourself to be happy without feeling guilty.
- Be kind to yourself.
- Reach out to others.

ACTIVITY 8.4 – READ

Read this case study and answer the questions that follow.

Case study

Kai is a 16-year-old teenager facing challenges in finding happiness and maintaining a positive outlook on life. Kai comes from a supportive family and attends a good secondary school. However, they have recently been experiencing stress and low self-esteem, and feel a lack of enthusiasm for daily activities. They have difficulty connecting with peers and often isolate themselves. Their parents and teachers are concerned about their emotional wellbeing and are looking for ways to improve Kai's happiness journey.

1. What has Kai been experiencing lately? How do they feel?
2. How can Kai's family play a role in supporting Kai's happiness journey?
3. Are there things in Kai's life that they can feel grateful for?
4. What can Kai do to improve their happiness journey?
5. What role can peer support and friendships play in improving Kai's happiness journey?

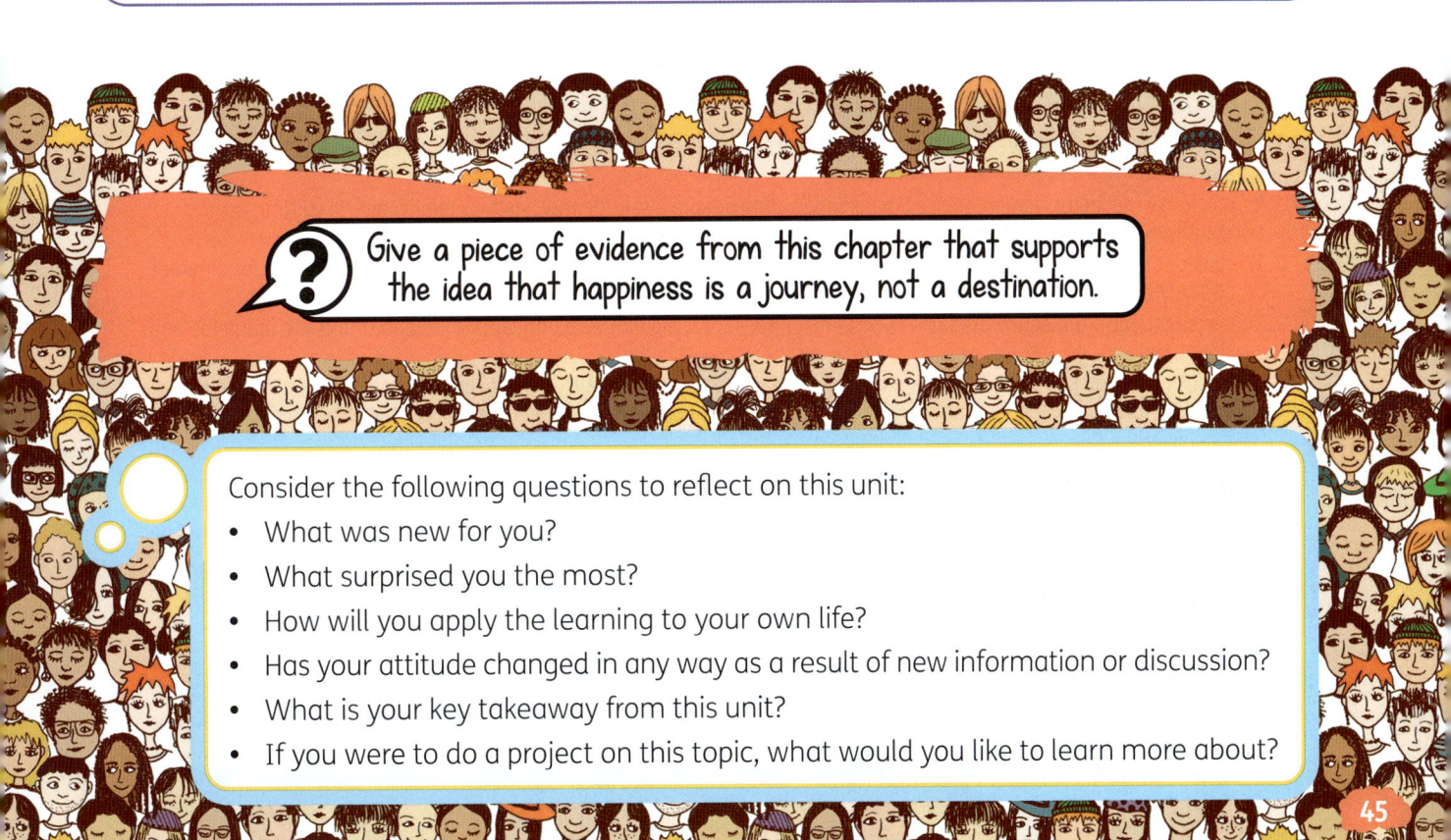

> Give a piece of evidence from this chapter that supports the idea that happiness is a journey, not a destination.

Consider the following questions to reflect on this unit:
- What was new for you?
- What surprised you the most?
- How will you apply the learning to your own life?
- Has your attitude changed in any way as a result of new information or discussion?
- What is your key takeaway from this unit?
- If you were to do a project on this topic, what would you like to learn more about?

UNIT OF LEARNING 2

Caring for My Mind and Body

The chapters in this Unit of Learning are:
- Chapter 9 – What Is Within and Beyond Our Control?
- Chapter 10 – Mastering Resilience in Challenging Times
- Chapter 11 – Coping Tools to Enhance Resilience
- Chapter 12 – Building a Positive Relationship with Food
- Chapter 13 – Disordered Eating Behaviours
- Chapter 14 – The Effects of Edited Images

Note for teachers: This Unit of Learning engages with the following Learning Outcomes:

1.3 explore the range of influences and life experiences that can impact on self-image and self-esteem and identify ways to nurture a positive sense of self-worth

1.4 recognise the factors and influences that shape young people's self-identity, such as family, peers, culture, gender identity, sexual orientation, race/ethnic background, dis/abilities, religious beliefs/world-views

2.1 consider the multifaceted nature of health and wellbeing, and evaluate what being healthy might look like for different adolescents, including how food, physical activity, sleep/rest and hygiene contribute to health and wellbeing

2.2 investigate how unhealthy products such as nicotine, vapes, alcohol, and unhealthy food and drinks are marketed and advertised

2.3 discuss societal, cultural and economic influences affecting young people when it comes to making healthy choices about smoking, alcohol and other addictive substances and behaviours, and how harmful influences can be overcome in real-life situations

2.6 consider scenarios where, for example, alcohol, nicotine, drugs, food and electronic devices might be used to cope with unpleasant feelings or stress, and discuss possible healthy ways of coping

2.10 demonstrate how to access and appraise appropriate and trustworthy information, supports and services about health and wellbeing

3.2 examine benefits and difficulties experienced by young people in a range of relationships – friendships, family relationships, and romantic/intimate relationships

4.2 recognise and acknowledge their emotions and recognise the links between thoughts, feelings and behaviour

4.4 discuss ways to support themselves and others in challenging times and where/how/when to seek support, if needed

4.5 explore how emotional wellbeing can be affected by factors within our control, such as sleep, diet, exercise, substance use and online exposure, and factors beyond our control

Related Learning Outcomes: 4.2, 4.4, 4.5.

CHAPTER 9

What Is Within and Beyond Our Control?

In this chapter we will:
- explore the different things in life that are within and beyond our control
- learn about painful emotions and feelings and how to deal with them
- discuss ways we can cope with things beyond our control when they occur.

KEY TERMS
Circle of control
Autopilot

? 'When you can't control what is happening, challenge yourself to control the way you respond to what is happening – that is where your power is.' What do you think this quote means?

Circle of control

Life is full of ups and downs. Sometimes, it can feel like we have no control over what's happening, and this can be very stressful. There are factors both within our control and beyond our control that influence our lives and wellbeing.

Factors within our control include our:
- thoughts
- choices
- actions.

We have the power to shape our attitudes, make positive decisions and take care of ourselves.

Factors beyond our control include:
- external events
- other people's actions
- circumstances we can't change.

Understanding that there are some things we can't control is important. It helps us to find resilience in the face of challenges, as we can focus on the things we can change.

A **circle of control** is a visual tool that helps us understand what we have control over in life and what we don't. It represents our level of influence over factors that affect us. The circle of control includes three circles:

No control
This circle represents the factors that are beyond our control, such as the actions of others, natural disasters or global events. These factors may cause worry or anxiety but are beyond our direct influence.

Some control
This circle represents the factors that we can indirectly affect, such as our relationships, communities or environments. While we may not have complete control over these factors, our actions and decisions can make a difference.

Most control
This circle represents the factors that we have the power to change or influence through our actions, choices and attitudes.

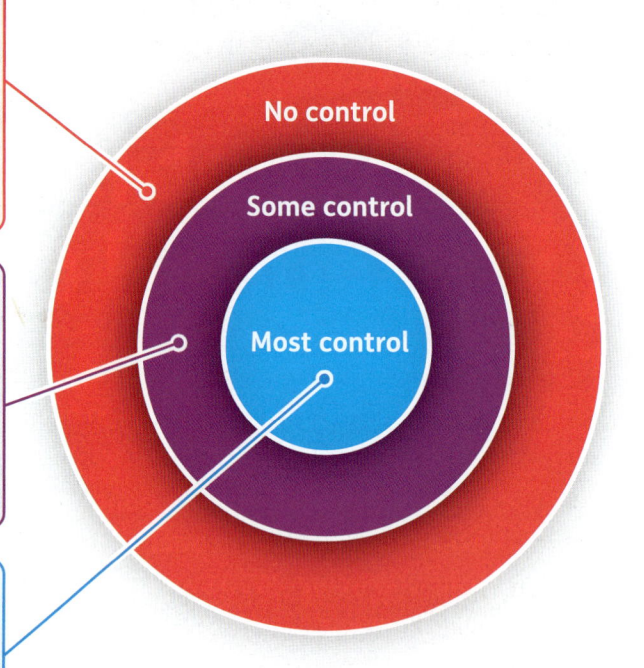

ACTIVITY 9.1 – THINK

A. In pairs, think about the circle of control and identify things that you feel you have:
- most control over
- some control over
- no control over.

B. Reflection questions:
1. Are there more things in life that we can control than we can't control?
2. How do factors beyond our control influence our overall wellbeing?
3. How can focusing on factors within our control help us to navigate challenges and maintain our wellbeing?
4. Are there ways to use the factors within our control to reduce the impact of factors beyond our control?

Painful emotions and feelings

Facing factors beyond our control can be incredibly challenging if we lack healthy coping strategies to lean on. Such situations can give rise to a range of painful emotions and feelings, including:

- fear
- anger
- hopelessness
- frustration
- helplessness
- anxiety.

Healthy coping tools are essential for handling upsetting events beyond our control. These tools act as a buffer against life's challenges and help protect our emotional wellbeing.

Painful emotions and feelings can be compared to ocean waves:

Imagine you are at the beach, and you wade into the sea until the water reaches your chest. As you stand there, you notice that the waves are steadily approaching the shore. If you try to resist the waves and prevent them from reaching their destination, you quickly realise their immense power. They push against you, overwhelming and engulfing. If you're not careful, they can sweep you off your feet.

Painful emotions and feelings are much like these waves. They can be powerful and quickly overwhelm us. The more we panic and fight against them, the harder it is to stay afloat. However, if we remain calm, brace ourselves and focus on keeping our head above the water, we can regain our footing. The fear of painful emotions often lasts until we give ourselves permission to experience them. When we do, we realise that they ebb and flow, much like waves.

All emotions and feelings are real and valid. They are the brain's way of making sense of the world, and they help us to survive. Instead of suppressing them or pushing them away, we can approach them with curiosity and use them to learn and grow.

'You can't stop the waves, but you can learn to surf.' – *Jon Kabat-Zinn*

It may sound simple, but having awareness can help us to understand and deal with our emotions. By switching off from **autopilot** (doing something without thinking about it) and working on increasing our awareness of our thoughts, emotions and urges, we can pause and think before acting.

ACTIVITY 9.2 – THINK

Think about the following questions and note down your reflections in your copy.

1. Do you have a habit of blocking out painful emotions and feelings?
2. What tools do you use to do this?
3. What might be the negative effects of doing this?
4. Are there alternative tools you could use to handle these emotions and feelings?

ACTIVITY 9.3 – READ

In pairs, read these four case studies and answer the questions that follow.

Case study 1: Managing stress

Sophie is juggling her schoolwork, extracurricular activities and part-time work. She notices that stress is taking a toll on her mental and physical health. She is finding it hard to fall asleep at night and is eating more.

Sophie decides to prioritise self-care by adding breathing techniques, exercise and regular breaks into her schedule. She also seeks support from friends and family and learns to improve her time management skills so that she doesn't feel as overwhelmed with her workload.

1. What factors are within Sophie's control for managing her stress?
2. How does Sophie demonstrate self-awareness and self-care practices?
3. How does Sophie's approach impact her stress levels and overall wellbeing?
4. What can you learn from Sophie's strategies for managing stress?

Case study 2: Coping with loss

Michael experiences the sudden loss of a close family member. He goes through a range of emotions, including grief and sadness. Michael acknowledges his feelings, seeks support from loved ones and engages in healthy coping mechanisms, including talking to a counsellor. He allows himself time to heal and adjust to life after the loss.

1. What factors are beyond Michael's control in this scenario?
2. How does Michael demonstrate resilience?
3. How do Michael's coping strategies contribute to his healing process?
4. What can you learn from Michael's approach to navigating loss and grief?

Case study 3: Unexpected break-up

Emily and Liam have been in a relationship for eight months. Suddenly, Liam informs Emily that he wants to end the relationship, without giving a clear explanation why. Emily is left feeling shocked, hurt and confused. Despite the unexpected nature of the break-up, Emily chooses to focus on her own wellbeing. She seeks support from friends and engages in self-care activities to heal and rebuild her life. In addition to her other coping tools, she finds daily affirmations (short, repeated phrases) like 'I am loved' and 'I deserve to be treated better' helpful for getting over her ex.

1. What factors are beyond Emily's control in this scenario?
2. How does Emily navigate the break-up despite it being a challenging situation?
3. How does Emily's focus on self-care and seeking support help her healing process?
4. What can you learn from Emily's decision to prioritise her wellbeing after a break-up?

Case study 4: Building self-confidence

Aiden struggles with low self-confidence and often feels overwhelmed by self-doubt. He decides to take charge of his self-esteem by engaging in gratitude practices daily, celebrating his achievements and setting realistic goals. Aiden also seeks support from a counsellor to work through his insecurities and develop a more positive self-image.

1. What factors are within Aiden's control for building his self-confidence?
2. How does Aiden demonstrate self-reflection?
3. How do Aiden's efforts impact his self-esteem and overall wellbeing?
4. What can you learn from Aiden's journey towards improving self-confidence?

TIPS

Here are some tips for coping with strong or painful emotions and feelings:

- **Identification:** Learn to identify how you're feeling. It can be easy to understand that you're sad or angry, but it helps to break these emotions down further. For example, you could feel distressed or inadequate, irritated or bitter. Linking the emotion or feeling to body sensations can help.

- **Self-soothing:** When a painful emotion or feeling becomes intense, it can feel like it's at its peak (highest wave) for a very long time. This can lead to the strong urge to do something unhealthy to make it disappear, such as binge eat or overexercise. When this happens, the best thing to do is to soothe yourself through your senses. For example, you could move your body, listen to calming music, talk to a trusted friend, breathe slowly and deeply, or smell a fragrance. One of the quickest ways to tell your brain that you are safe is actually through your sense of smell!

- **Mindset:** The way we perceive a situation can strongly affect how we handle it. With a growth mindset (the belief that our skills and abilities can develop and change), we shift from feeling defeated to finding solutions. It empowers us to be resilient.

- **Affirmations:** Use positive affirmations to help you cope with painful emotions and feelings. These affirmations can improve your mood, help you feel more resilient and allow you to see the positive side of a difficult situation.

- **Support:** Seek support from your friends or family, or talk to a counsellor if you are struggling with very painful emotions and feelings.

? The next time you are dealing with something beyond your control, what might you do differently?

Related Learning Outcomes: 2.6, 3.2, 4.2, 4.4.

CHAPTER 10

Mastering Resilience in Challenging Times

In this chapter we will:
- explore what it means to have resilience
- learn about the executive brain and the autopilot brain
- discover how to build resilience by engaging the executive brain
- reflect on how we have engaged our executive brains in challenging situations.

KEY TERMS
Resilience
Executive brain
Autopilot brain
Adaptability

? Identify two things you remember learning about resilience in previous years.

What can resilience do?

Resilience is the ability to believe in yourself, to cope to the best of your abilities, and to adapt well in difficult circumstances. Remember, resilience is not a trait that you either have or don't have. Instead, it's a set of behaviours, thoughts and actions that you can learn and develop at any time.

You will encounter many challenges in your life, from fights with friends to setbacks in your schoolwork or hobbies. Having resilience allows you to rebound and learn from these challenges. When you have resilience, you are equipped to explore new paths to reaching your goals.

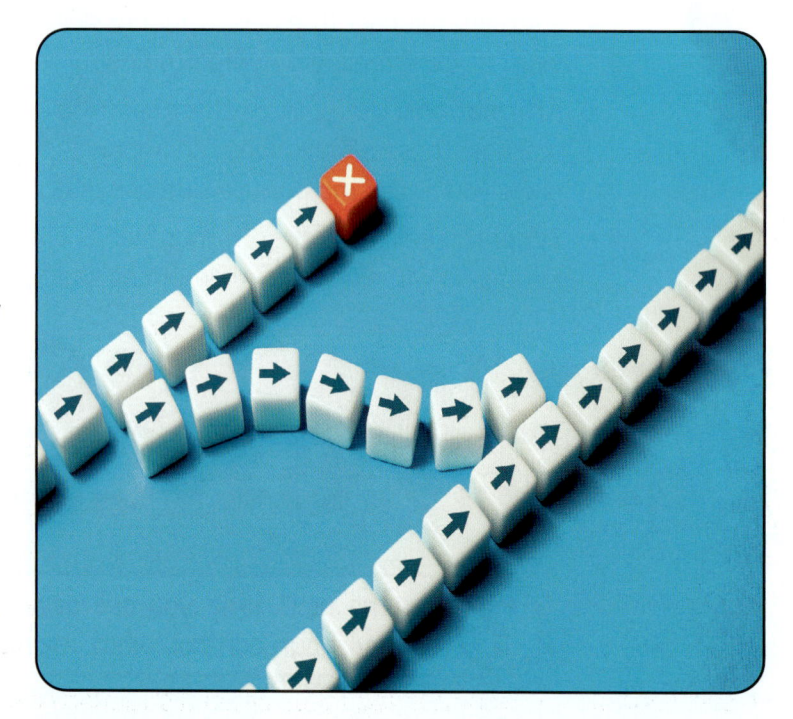

ACTIVITY 10.1 – WATCH

A. Watch this video about the challenges that athlete Asha Philip had to overcome and reflect on the questions that follow.

▶ www.educate*plus*.ie/go/asha-philip

1. 'Some people say you have to be broken to be fixed again.' Do you agree with this statement?
2. Asha says that 'in a heartbeat, everything was just gone' after she broke her leg. What feelings do you think Asha was experiencing in the moments and days following this accident?
3. How do you think Asha felt after being told that she was a 'write off'?
4. Asha wanted to give up, but she didn't. Why didn't she?
5. How would you describe Asha's mentality?
6. 'The only thing standing between success and failure is mental toughness.' Do you agree with this statement?

B. Read this account of Asha's recovery. Comment on the role that resilience played in her future successes.

Asha Philip's recovery

Asha endured three years of rigorous rehabilitation following her injuries at the 2007 World Championships. Her aspiration of representing Great Britain in the 2008 Olympic Games vanished, and her hopes were further shattered when a hamstring problem prevented her from competing for a spot on the London 2012 team, after she had decided to concentrate on athletics.

After a long wait of seven years, Asha's hard work paid off. She won silver in the 4 × 200 m relay in the 2014 World Relays and secured European gold in the 4 × 100 m relay. In addition, Asha, along with Bianca Williams, Jodie Williams and Ashleigh Nelson, represented England in the Commonwealth Games in Glasgow, where they won a bronze medal.

Building resilience

When you are faced with something new or challenging in life, you have to focus on every detail and task in order to overcome it. In Asha's case, she had to pay close attention to:

- every negative word that she was saying to herself
- every movement she took
- every rehabilitation exercise she had to perform.

This process can be very exhausting, as it relies on **the executive brain**, which is the part of the brain responsible for:

- planning
- flexible thinking
- goal setting
- multitasking
- self-control
- maintaining focus when distractions exist.

When we repeat a task over time, it is passed over to the **autopilot brain**. This means that the task is completed automatically, which requires less mental effort. This takes some of the strain off the executive brain. In other words, the longer you repeat a task, the easier it becomes.

When you consciously approach difficulties using your executive brain, you're better equipped to find solutions to setbacks. Meanwhile, relying on your autopilot brain for everyday routines helps to free up mental resources for important decisions. This balance enhances your ability to manage stress, make positive choices and maintain overall wellbeing, contributing to greater levels of resilience.

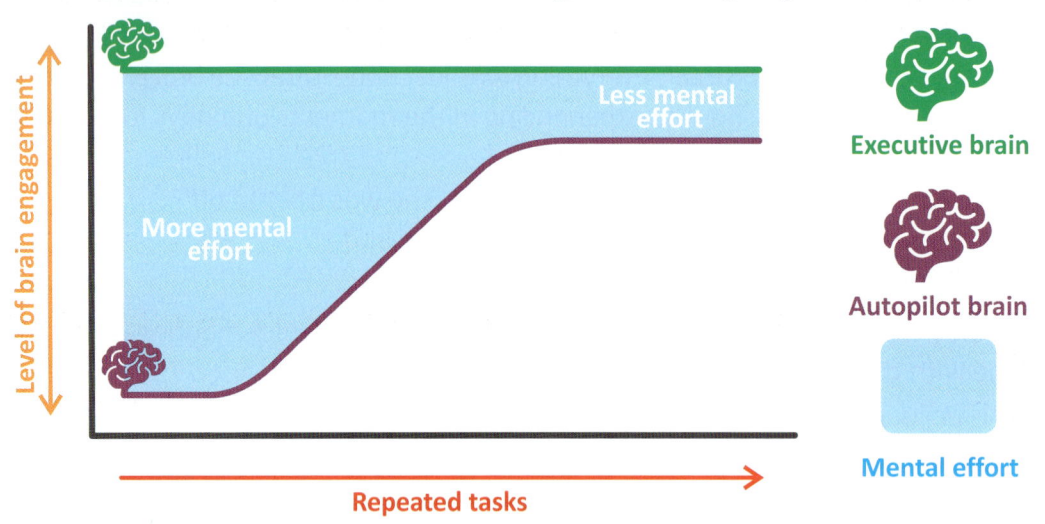

ACTIVITY 10.2 – READ

Read this case study about building resilience by engaging the executive brain and answer the questions that follow.

Case study

Ethan is 16 years old. He recently went through a break-up with his partner, which significantly affected his emotional wellbeing. The break-up left Ethan feeling overwhelmed and emotionally drained. For a time, Ethan struggled with school performance, and his interactions with friends and family were affected. However, he was determined to build his resilience and find ways to navigate through this challenging time.

To do this, Ethan began to engage his executive brain in the following ways:

Planning and goal setting: Ethan realised the importance of setting goals to stay focused and motivated during this difficult period. He decided to improve his academic performance and invest time in a new hobby, which provided a sense of purpose and achievement.

Understanding emotions: Ethan learned to recognise and accept his emotions, understanding that it's normal to feel hurt after a break-up. He found this helpful in managing his painful emotions.

> **Adaptability** (the ability to adjust to changes in your environment): Ethan worked on being more adaptable and used his logical thinking to approach the situation. He identified what he could and couldn't control about the break-up and focused on what was within his control, such as his reactions and personal growth.
>
> **Building support systems:** Ethan actively reached out to trusted friends and family members to communicate his feelings as he navigated through his break-up.

1. How did engaging his executive brain help Ethan on his resilience-building journey? How will it affect Ethan's emotional wellbeing?
2. If Ethan instead chose to isolate himself and distract himself with social media, what might have been the outcome?
3. Do you think that the more Ethan engages in these practices, the easier they will become to do? Why?

ACTIVITY 10.3 – CREATE

CBA 1

Recall a challenging situation you faced in the past two years, such as:
- studying for a difficult exam
- fighting with a friend
- going through a break-up.

Thinking about the situation, consider the following questions:

1. What tasks did you have to engage in consciously and repeatedly to overcome the situation? (Executive brain)
2. How did these tasks become more automatic over time? (Autopilot brain)

Using your answers from the questions above, create a diagram similar to the one below. Fill in the sections to illustrate the difficult tasks you initially engaged in, and how they gradually became easier and more automatic as time passed. An example has been done for you:

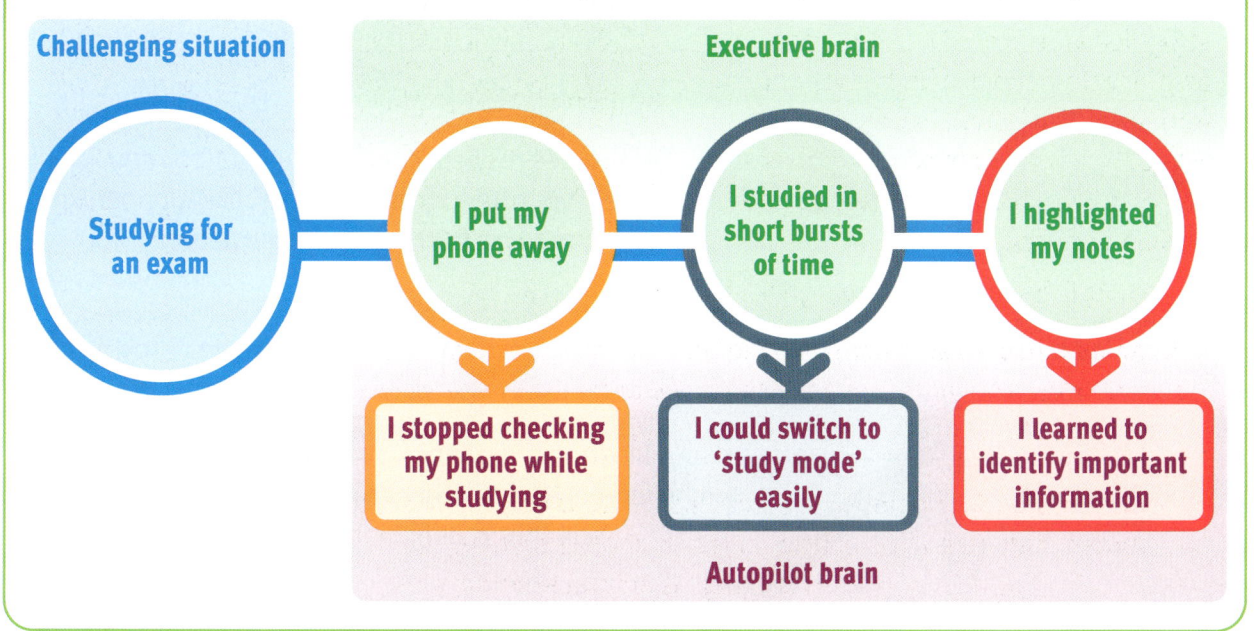

Challenging situation: Studying for an exam

Executive brain:
- I put my phone away
- I studied in short bursts of time
- I highlighted my notes

Autopilot brain:
- I stopped checking my phone while studying
- I could switch to 'study mode' easily
- I learned to identify important information

Building resilience is hard

Because the brain seeks comfort, it often wants to avoid the difficult parts of building resilience. However, facing challenges and stepping out of your comfort zone is necessary for building resilience. This allows you to:

- learn
- grow
- become stronger at overcoming obstacles.

Pushing through your discomfort will strengthen your ability to deal with bigger and more difficult challenges that arise in the future.

ACTIVITY 10.4 – DISCUSS

A. The following idioms have been used to describe resilience. (An idiom is a saying or phrase that is used to describe a situation.) Read through each idiom and its meaning and choose the one that you feel best describes resilience. Pair up with the person beside you and discuss the reason behind your choice.

Idiom	Meaning
Bouncing back	Illustrates resilience as the ability to quickly recover from challenges, like a ball bouncing back after being dropped.
Rolling with the punches	Portrays resilience as the ability to adapt to difficult situations and keep going, similar to a boxer who can absorb punches and continue fighting.
Rising from the ashes	Symbolises resilience as the capacity to rebuild and recover after a major setback, like a phoenix emerging from its own destruction.
Tough as nails	Illustrates resilience as the ability to endure challenging circumstances and remain strong, like a nail that is difficult to bend or break.

CHAPTER 10 – MASTERING RESILIENCE IN CHALLENGING TIMES

Idiom	Meaning
Bending, but not breaking	Represents resilience as the ability to adapt to change without being permanently damaged, like a flexible tree that can withstand strong winds without breaking.
Weather the storm	Portrays resilience as the capacity to endure difficult circumstances and come out unscathed, like a ship that can withstand rough seas and navigate through a storm.
Ride the waves	Symbolises resilience as the ability to cope with fluctuating circumstances and challenges, like a surfer who rides the waves of the ocean.
Going the distance	Represents resilience as the ability to persevere and stay committed even when faced with challenges or setbacks, like a marathon runner who keeps going despite the difficulties of the race.
Getting back on the horse	Symbolises resilience as the ability to get up after falling or failing, like a rider who falls off a horse but gets back on and keeps riding.

B. Using your chosen idiom, write a short personal message to remind yourself of the importance of staying resilient when times are tough.

? Starting today, what specific action or task can you commit to that will help you build your resilience by engaging your executive brain?

57

Related Learning Outcomes: 1.3, 4.2, 4.4.

CHAPTER 11

Coping Tools to Enhance Resilience

In this chapter we will:
- learn about the relationship between resilience and coping tools
- identify particular coping tools that work best in different situations
- recognise that everyone requires different coping tools to overcome challenges
- appreciate that anxiety is a common feeling that everyone experiences in life
- consider the importance of exposing ourselves to situations that cause anxiety.

KEY TERMS
Coping tools
Anxiety

? Who comes to mind when you think of a resilient person? Why?

The relationship between resilience and coping tools

Resilience isn't always constant. People's levels of resilience vary to different degrees, depending on their stages in life and the challenges they face. For example, someone may be very resilient in school, but may not be as resilient in their personal life or relationships. In other words, a person's level of resilience can depend on the situation at hand.

Because resilience can fluctuate, coping tools can be used to enhance resilience in times of difficulty. **Coping tools** are tools that help us manage stressors and navigate tough situations. In First Year, we learned that they can be:

- **Problem based:** These target stressors in practical ways (setting goals, asking for support, etc.).
- **Emotion based:** These help us to deal with negative emotional responses to stressors (exercising, meditating, etc.).

CHAPTER 11 – COPING TOOLS TO ENHANCE RESILIENCE

Certain coping tools can work brilliantly in some situations and not so well in others. Figuring out which coping tools to use in a challenging situation is crucial for enhancing our resilience and looking after our emotional wellbeing. The wrong coping tool can make an unpleasant experience more difficult to deal with.

ACTIVITY 11.1 – READ

In pairs, read through the situations that Frankie and Dale go through and answer the questions that follow.

Frankie

Situation 1:
Frankie has her Junior Cycle exams coming up, and the pressure is intense. To cope, she turns to her journal, writing down her fears, doubts and frustrations. Expressing herself through writing helps her release stress and gain clarity. It also brings her a sense of relief and allows her to approach her studies with renewed focus and a positive mindset.

Situation 2:
Frankie has a major fight with one of her friends, leaving her hurt and angry. She turns to her journal, hoping it will help like before. However, she realises that writing alone can't fix the conflict or mend their relationship. Recognising the need for guidance, Frankie decides to talk things out with her older sister and get advice on how to move forward.

Dale

Situation 1:
Dale is overwhelmed by a demanding academic workload, which is affecting their emotional wellbeing. Whenever the pressure builds up, Dale relies on physical exercise to relieve stress. Hitting the gym or going for a long run becomes an outlet for them, helping them to clear their mind and regain focus on their studies.

Situation 2:
Dale finds themselves in an argument with their boyfriend, leaving them very upset. To cope, Dale turns to intense physical exercise, as they had done in the past. However, this time they realise that exercise alone can't resolve the argument. They still feel stressed and worried even after an intense workout. Dale decides that the best way to resolve the fight with their boyfriend is to talk it out when they have both calmed down.

1. How does the effectiveness of Frankie and Dale's chosen coping tools differ between the situations they face?
2. Are there more effective coping tools Frankie and Dale could have used for dealing with the specific challenges they encountered?
3. What did Frankie and Dale learn about the importance of adapting their coping strategies to different situations?

ACTIVITY 11.2 – THINK

A. Reflect individually on a recent challenging situation you faced. Write down the coping tool(s) you used and how effective they were in that specific scenario.

B. Share your reflections in small groups and discuss how different situations may require different coping tools.

ACTIVITY 11.3 – DISCUSS

In pairs, discuss and brainstorm coping tools that would be most effective for each of the following scenarios. Your teacher will present you with a set of coping tools to help you with this.

Dealing with a disagreement with a close friend.	Coping with your partner ending your relationship.
Coming out as gay to a friend, who does not respond in the way you had hoped.	Questioning your sexual orientation.
Facing a challenging academic assignment or project at school.	Coping with a family conflict or tension at home.
Managing feelings of anxiety before a big test or presentation.	Handling a disappointment or setback, such as not getting a desired role in a play or not making a sports team.
Coping with the loss of a loved one.	Navigating a change or transition, such as moving to a new school.
Dealing with overwhelming stress from schoolwork, extracurricular activities and other commitments.	Managing feelings of loneliness or isolation.
Handling negative self-talk or low self-esteem.	Supporting a friend who is being called names for wearing their hijab.
Helping a classmate with a disability who is struggling with classwork.	Supporting a family member or friend who is experiencing mental health challenges.

Anxiety: Something we all experience

> **Anxiety** is a feeling of unease or worry that is often accompanied by physical symptoms such as an increased heart rate, restlessness, shallow breathing and a tightness in the chest.

| Anxiety is common when facing challenging situations. Our minds and bodies see these situations as potential threats, and anxiety is a natural response designed to keep us safe. | However, it's important to remember that anxiety doesn't define us, and we have the power to manage it. | By understanding that anxiety is a normal reaction, we can learn to manage it. |

Gradually exposing ourselves to anxiety-provoking situations:
- helps build up our ability to handle discomfort
- boosts our confidence and shows us that we can handle challenging situations
- allows us to become more adaptable, confident and equipped to cope with anything.

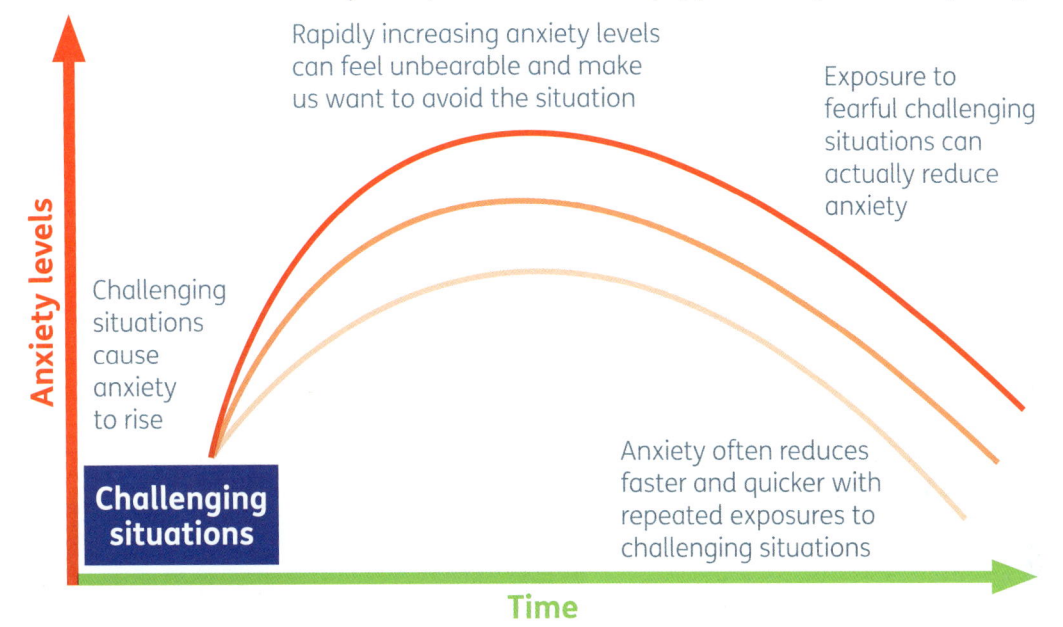

Anxiety levels (y-axis) vs **Time** (x-axis)

- Challenging situations cause anxiety to rise
- Rapidly increasing anxiety levels can feel unbearable and make us want to avoid the situation
- Exposure to fearful challenging situations can actually reduce anxiety
- Anxiety often reduces faster and quicker with repeated exposures to challenging situations

Not everyone will experience anxiety in the same way. While occasional anxiety is a normal part of life, it's vital to distinguish it from anxiety disorder, which is a mental illness that can be severe.

ACTIVITY 11.4 – WATCH

Watch this short film about anxiety and answer the questions that follow.

▶ www.educate*plus*.ie/go/anxiety-short-film

1. How does Madeline's internal voice affect her anxiety levels?
2. What helps Madeline overcome these negative thoughts?
3. If Madeline continued to listen to these internal thoughts and isolated herself further from her friends, how might this affect her emotional wellbeing?
4. How does anxiety affect your thoughts, emotions and physical sensations when you face a challenging situation?
5. Are there any common triggers or situations that cause you to feel anxious?
6. Can you think of a time when you felt particularly anxious about a situation? Did you avoid the situation or expose yourself to it? What was the outcome?
7. Reflecting on the previous activities, what coping tools have you found helpful in managing feelings of anxiety?

ACTIVITY 11.5 – THINK

The following quotes relate to anxiety. Choose one that resonates with you and reflect on the reasons why. Write down these reasons in your copy.

'Mantra for anxiety: This is not you. It is something moving through you. It can leave out the same door that it came in.' – James Clear

'Although anxiety is part of life, never let it control you.' – Paulo Coelho

'Slow breathing is like an anchor in the midst of an emotional storm: the anchor won't make the storm go away, but it will hold you steady until it passes.' – Russ Harris

'Don't believe the things you tell yourself late at night.' – Cheryl

ACTIVITY 11.6 – DISCUSS

A. In groups, brainstorm and make a list of different healthy coping tools teenagers can use in times of stress or difficulty. Decide on which coping tool you think is the most effective, for example, mindfulness, journaling, physical exercise or creative expression.

B. In the same groups, plan a workshop focused on resilience for teenagers. In your workshop, you should include information about what resilience means to you, why it's important for teenagers, and how teenagers can show resilience. Your workshop should include information about the importance and benefits of using healthy coping tools. Use your chosen coping tool from part A as an example, providing information about why it's beneficial and how it can help build resilience.

C. Present your workshop to your class. Engage in discussions about how resilience can promote good emotional wellbeing.

? How could using resilience and coping tools make a positive difference in your life? How might you apply these tools to challenging situations?

Related Learning Outcomes: 2.2, 2.3, 2.10.

CHAPTER 12

Building a Positive Relationship with Food

In this chapter we will:
- consider what a positive relationship with food involves
- explore the meaning of the term 'food addiction'
- research the claims in favour of and against the concept of food addiction
- consider the challenges to making healthy food choices
- examine the importance of a balanced diet.

KEY TERMS
Addiction
Food addiction
Endorsements

? In your opinion, what does a positive relationship with food look and feel like?

A positive relationship with food

A positive relationship with food involves:
- trying out different types of foods, without unnecessary restrictions
- recognising the value of food beyond just calories
- listening to your body's signals for hunger and fullness
- refraining from viewing food as a reward for exercise
- focusing on the abundance of foods you can eat, rather than on what you shouldn't.

Each person's positive relationship with food will be unique to them. It should meet their nutritional needs and provide comfort and satisfaction.

Is food addiction real?

Addiction is the repeated consumption of a substance despite the harm it causes to a person's health and wellbeing. **Food addiction** is a term that some researchers use to describe obsessive eating habits, which may be similar to addiction-like behaviours.

63

The concept of food addiction is a controversial topic in the medical world:

Some people believe that certain foods can make us feel addicted, leading to unhealthy eating habits. They argue that these foods can trigger strong cravings and make it hard to control how much we eat. They use the term 'food addiction' to describe this.

However, others disagree and say that this not a real addiction. They argue that there isn't sufficient evidence to prove that food can be as addictive as drugs and other substances. They think that food consumption has more to do with personal choices and habits, rather than being something we can't control.

The debate is ongoing, and researchers are still trying to figure out the truth.

ACTIVITY 12.1 – DISCUSS

In groups, research a variety of reliable websites and articles that argue for and against the existence of food addiction. Present your findings to the class. Use the following questions to support your research:

Arguing for the existence of food addiction

1. What scientific studies support the reality of food addiction?
2. How do these studies define and measure food addiction?
3. What are the main findings and evidence from these studies?
4. Which specific foods or components (e.g. sugar, fat, salt) are commonly associated with addictive behaviours?
5. How does the brain's reward system and dopamine release relate to food addiction?
6. Are there any similarities between food addiction and other substance addictions?

Arguing against the existence of food addiction

1. What are the main arguments against the existence of food addiction?
2. How do critics define the addictive properties of certain foods?
3. What are the criticisms of the scientific studies supporting food addiction?
4. Are there alternative explanations for addictive-like behaviours towards food (e.g. psychological factors, societal factors)?
5. How can personal responsibility and choice help us understand food consumption and cravings?
6. What are the roles of cultural, environmental and socio-economic factors in shaping food preferences and eating behaviours?

Challenges to making healthy food choices

While the debate around food addiction goes on, what is clear is that making healthy food choices can be challenging for teenagers, due to various factors:

Peer pressure and the desire to fit in may lead to the consumption of less nutritious foods, such as fast food or sugary snacks.

CHAPTER 12 – BUILDING A POSITIVE RELATIONSHIP WITH FOOD

> Limited access to nutritious food options in certain environments, such as at school or at home, can affect a teenager's ability to make healthy food choices.

> Lack of knowledge about nutrition and the skills to prepare healthy meals can further complicate decision making.

> Food advertisements are everywhere. They're designed to grab people's attention and make them want certain foods. Constant exposure to food advertisements, particularly those featuring celebrity **endorsements** (approval or support), can influence teenagers' preferences and promote less nutritious eating. A study found that teenagers see marketing for food between 30 and 189 times per week on social media apps, with fast food and sugary drinks being the most common. According to the same study, young people who were exposed to vloggers (people who regularly post short videos) promoting sugary and fatty snacks went on to eat 26 per cent more calories than those who weren't.

Making unhealthy food choices is putting young teenagers at higher risk of health issues such as obesity, type 2 diabetes and heart complications.

ACTIVITY 12.2 – WATCH

Watch these food and drink advertisements that feature celebrity endorsements. Then answer the questions below for each advertisement.

▶ www.educate*plus*.ie/go/diet-coke-ad

▶ www.educate*plus*.ie/go/mcdonalds-ad

▶ www.educate*plus*.ie/go/tim-hortons-ad

1. What emotions or feelings does the advertisement evoke? *looking*
2. Does the advertisement make you feel positive, inspired or drawn towards the product? Why? *no*
3. What do you know about the celebrity endorsing the product? Are they known for their expertise in nutrition or health? *no*
4. How does the celebrity's presence in the advertisement influence your perception of the product's healthiness or effectiveness? *it doesn't*
5. How is the product's packaging or presentation designed to appeal to consumers (catchy slogans, design, celebrity credibility)?

ACTIVITY 12.3 – CREATE (CBA 1)

Many celebrities endorse highly processed foods, but you are about to change this!

Imagine that you are part of a marketing team promoting healthy eating habits. In groups, choose a well-known celebrity and develop a campaign in which the celebrity promotes nutritious foods or healthy lifestyle choices. Create a poster or advertisement showcasing the celebrity endorsing healthy options and emphasising the benefits of making nutritious choices.

Present your campaign to the class, explaining why you believe your chosen celebrity is a good fit and how your campaign aims to positively influence food choices.

The importance of a balanced diet

A balanced diet involves eating a combination of foods that provide essential nutrients and nourishment. In First Year, we learned that for teenagers, this means consuming the following per day:

Protein (46 to 52 g)

Fat (56 to 78 g)

Fibre (25 to 30 g)

Carbohydrates (120 g)

Water (six to eight glasses)

Eating a balanced diet makes you feel full and satisfied throughout the day and also improves concentration. This can reduce food cravings and the effects of factors such as peer pressure and food advertisements, ultimately leading to a healthier lifestyle.

Remember, treats are also a part of a balanced diet – no food is off limits. However, it's advisable to consume these treats in moderation.

ACTIVITY 12.4 – DISCUSS

In groups, you will be assigned one of the following food groups that contributes to a balanced diet:

- Protein
- Fat (unsaturated)
- Carbohydrates
- Fibre

Research and discuss recipes, ingredients and ready-made snacks that contribute to meeting the daily requirements of your assigned food group. As a class, shares tips and ideas on how to achieve a balanced diet.

? Identify one barrier to building a positive relationship with food and outline how it can be overcome.

Related Learning Outcomes: 1.4, 2.1, 2.3, 2.6, 4.4.

CHAPTER 13

Disordered Eating Behaviours

In this chapter we will:
- identify behaviours that fall under disordered eating
- consider the spectrum of disordered eating behaviours
- reflect on our own relationships with food
- learn about the signs and symptoms of disordered eating behaviours
- learn about risk factors for disordered eating behaviours
- identify who to seek help from if we are concerned about our eating behaviours.

KEY TERMS
Disordered eating behaviours
Eating disorders
Fatphobia

? Do you think that the way we see ourselves and the foods we choose can affect our health and happiness? How?

What are disordered eating behaviours?

Disordered eating behaviours refer to a wide range of irregular eating behaviours that may negatively affect someone's physical, mental or emotional health. While disordered eating isn't considered an eating disorder by itself, people who engage in disordered eating are at high risk of developing eating disorders over time. **Eating disorders** are serious mental health conditions that involve unhealthy attitudes, behaviours and perceptions related to food, body image and weight.

67

Examples of disordered eating behaviours may include the following:

Avoiding certain food groups or macronutrients without a medical reason.

Binge-eating: This is when someone eats a lot of food in a short time and feels like they can't control it. It's often followed by feelings of distress or guilt.

Compensatory behaviours: These are actions or strategies that people use to compensate for the calories they have consumed, or to relieve feelings of guilt, anxiety or discomfort related to eating. Examples include skipping meals, tracking food intake and overexercising.

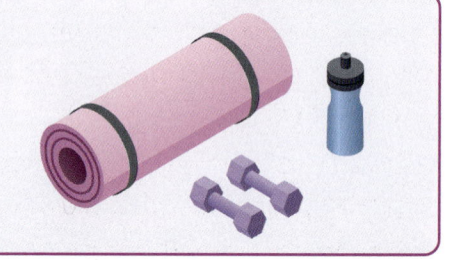

Fasting: This is when someone chooses not to eat or drink for a period of time.

Following strict food rules.

Obsessively tracking food or body measurements.

Participating in fad diets: These are trendy and often extreme eating plans that promise quick weight loss, but are not always based on balanced or sustainable nutrition.

Unfortunately, disordered eating behaviours are becoming more and more normalised in society today. When these behaviours are seen as 'normal', it can be harder for people to recognise that they are harmful. Over time, these behaviours can become more compulsive and fixed.

Identifying disordered eating behaviours can be complicated. For example:

- Fasting for weight loss may be disordered, but fasting for religious reasons is not necessarily harmful.
- Having strict 'food rules' may indicate disordered eating, but having preferences, dietary restrictions (e.g. gluten intolerance) or cultural eating practices is not the same.

Most cases of disordered eating are rooted in body image concerns, which are often influenced by fatphobia. **Fatphobia** refers to the unfair judgement or treatment of people because of their body size or weight, especially if they have larger bodies.

The weight loss industry, the media and social media influencers can promote behaviours and products meant to keep weights low and waistlines small. However, there is increasing evidence to suggest that weight loss diets do more harm than good for many people, and these diets can lead to disordered eating habits.

Spectrum of eating behaviours

Healthy eating   **Disordered eating**   **Eating disorder**

Disordered eating comes in a spectrum. Individuals who have a healthy relationship with food fall on one end, and individuals with diagnosed eating disorders fall on the other. Along this spectrum, disordered eating behaviours and attitudes towards food and body image range from mild to severe. For example:

- Occasional or infrequent disordered eating habits can be classified as mild. These behaviours can generally be addressed and overcome quickly.
- Diagnosed eating disorders that cause significant physical and psychological distress can be classified as severe. It may require significant time and resources to address and overcome these behaviours.

ACTIVITY 13.1 – READ

A. Read these four scenarios and identify where you believe each individual falls on the spectrum of eating behaviours. Label the diagram below with your answers.

Mary maintains a healthy relationship with food by enjoying a balanced diet and listening to her body's hunger and fullness cues. She has no restrictions or obsessions related to food and feels comfortable and satisfied with her eating habits.

Luka occasionally engages in emotional eating, using food as a coping mechanism when he feels stressed or upset. While it does not significantly impact his overall wellbeing, he recognises the need to address this behaviour and seeks support when needed.

Mirra follows strict dietary rules and avoids certain food groups, believing they are 'bad' or unhealthy. She constantly worries about her body shape and weight, which affects her self-esteem.

Tinna experiences frequent episodes of binge-eating. They also engage in compensatory behaviours such as excessive exercise to manage their weight. They isolate themselves to hide these behaviours, and this is starting to negatively affect their relationships.

Healthy eating   **Disordered eating**   **Eating disorder**

B. Reflection questions:
1. After considering the scenarios, which behaviours or attitudes stood out to you the most? Why do you think they were significant?
2. How do you think societal influences (e.g. the media and cultural expectations) contribute to the development of disordered eating behaviours?
3. How might these behaviours affect an individual's relationships and overall quality of life?
4. What are some warning signs that you would consider indicators of a problematic relationship with food?

C. Personal reflection: Reflect on your own eating habits and attitudes towards food. Do you see any similarities or differences with the examples provided in the scenarios? How would you describe your current relationship with food?

Signs and symptoms of disordered eating

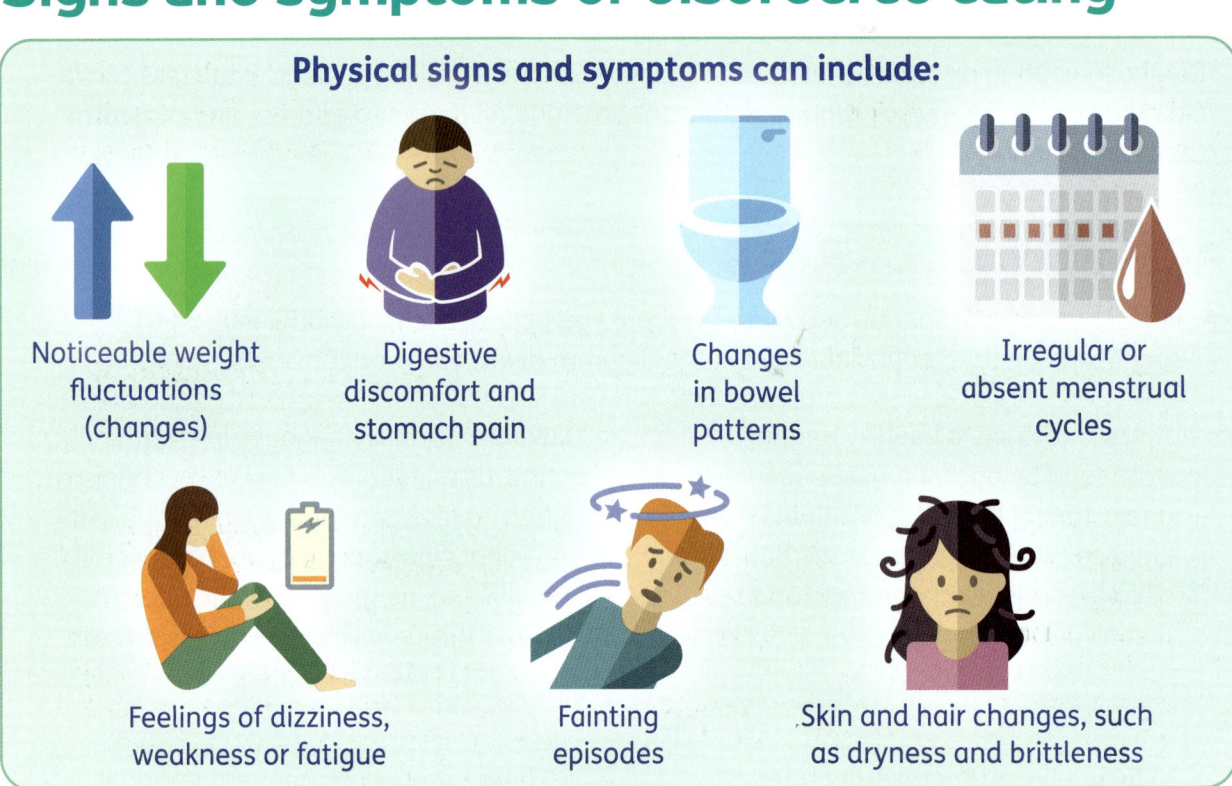

Physical signs and symptoms can include:

- Noticeable weight fluctuations (changes)
- Digestive discomfort and stomach pain
- Changes in bowel patterns
- Irregular or absent menstrual cycles
- Feelings of dizziness, weakness or fatigue
- Fainting episodes
- Skin and hair changes, such as dryness and brittleness

Emotional signs and symptoms can include:

- Excessive preoccupation with weight, food, diets, calories or carbohydrates, overshadowing other aspects of life
- Obsessive thoughts about body image, size, shape or specific body parts 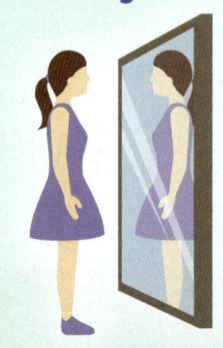
- Severely restricting food variety, eliminating whole food groups and only considering a limited range of foods 'safe' 
- Avoiding social eating occasions and withdrawing from such activities

Risks of disordered eating

People who experience disordered eating often underestimate or fail to recognise the harmful effects it can have on their mental and physical wellbeing. Some complications that can arise from disordered eating include:

- a greater risk of obesity and eating disorders
- bone loss
- digestive issues such as diarrhoea, bloating, gas, heartburn and nausea
- mineral imbalances, which can lead to issues like fatigue, headaches and constipation
- low heart rate and blood pressure
- increased anxiety
- depression and social isolation.

ACTIVITY 13.2 – DISCUSS

In pairs, imagine you are an Agony Aunt for a newspaper, offering advice to readers for their problems or queries. Read and discuss each of the Agony Aunt queries below. First, decide whether each query shows disordered eating behaviours or not. Then consider what advice you would offer each reader.

Ask *Auntie Anne*

Dear Auntie Anne,

I've recently started fasting to lose weight because I see others doing it and claiming it's effective. I skip meals or restrict my eating window, thinking it will help me shed kilograms, but it makes me feel dizzy and unfocused. I'm starting to worry if this is becoming disordered eating behaviour. Can you help me figure out if I should be concerned?

Sincerely,
Confused Faster

Dear Auntie Anne,

I've been avoiding carbs because I've heard they make you gain weight. I constantly check food labels, and if something has too many carbs, I won't eat it. Lately, I've started to feel guilty when I eat carbs, and it's affecting my social life. I avoid eating out with friends as it's too hard to control the amount of carbs that are in a meal. Could this be a sign of disordered eating?

Sincerely,
Carb-conscious

Dear Auntie Anne,

I'm genuinely concerned about developing disordered eating habits because I'm often self-conscious about my body and weight. Although I don't engage in extreme behaviours like fasting or restricting food, I worry that my thoughts are becoming unhealthy. What should I do to maintain a positive relationship with food and body image?

Sincerely,
Concerned Teen

Dear Auntie Anne,

Whenever I eat a meal, especially if I feel like I've overindulged, I feel this intense need to immediately burn off the calories through excessive exercise. I'm worried that this behaviour is becoming unhealthy and could be a sign of a larger problem. What should I do?

Sincerely,
Exercise-obsessed

Who is at risk of disordered eating behaviours?

- Teenagers who have poor body image are more at risk of developing disordered eating behaviours.
- Teenagers with high levels of perfectionism, particularly in relation to their body and weight, may be more prone to developing disordered eating behaviours.
- Society, the media and unrealistic beauty ideals can trigger unhealthy eating habits in those who believe and adopt these ideas.
- Peer groups that place a strong focus on appearance and dieting behaviours may influence teenagers to engage in disordered eating habits.
- Certain sports and performing arts that emphasise weight or body shape may put individuals at a higher risk of developing disordered eating behaviours.
- A family history of disordered eating or mental health conditions can increase the likelihood of an individual developing disordered eating patterns.

ACTIVITY 13.3 – THINK

Ask yourself these questions to determine whether you need help for disordered eating:

1. Do you use food to escape from stress?
2. Does the number on your weighing scale affect your thinking?
3. Are you constantly thinking of food?
4. Do you binge eat?

Note: If you answered 'yes' to any of these questions, it's important to seek support. The longer you wait, the greater the risk of these thoughts and behaviours becoming more deeply rooted and harder to change.

Here are some tips if you have concerns about your own eating habits or those of a loved one:
- Reach out to a professional who specialises in disordered eating.
- Don't hesitate to talk openly about any concerns.
- Prioritise self-care and positive body image.
- Seek a support system.

Here are some online supports that address disordered eating:
- **Bodywhys:** www.bodywhys.ie
- **HSE:** www2.hse.ie/mental-health/issues/eating-disorders
- **National Eating Disorders Recovery Centre:** www.nedrc.ie
- **Spunout:** www.spunout.ie

Remember, you're not alone. Seeking help and understanding is a sign of strength and resilience.

Give one example of a disordered eating behaviour and one example of a healthy eating behaviour.

Related Learning Outcomes: 1.3, 2.10.

CHAPTER 14

The Effects of Edited Images

In this chapter we will:

- ✓ explore what image editing is and how it is used on social media
- ✓ consider the impact of edited images on body image
- ✓ determine whether images of celebrities have been edited or not
- ✓ research online movements about edited images and body image.

KEY TERMS
Image editing
Airbrushing
Filtering

? Do you follow any famous people on social media? Do you know if any of them use edited images of themselves? How can you tell?

What is image editing?

Image editing refers to modifying photos or videos using different techniques, tools or software. Image editing can include:

Airbrushing, which refers to any retouching done on an image that changes the reality of the image. It may include removing people or objects, erasing flaws or altering body shapes. This can be done after the image is taken, in programs like Photoshop. Airbrushed images can appear in magazines, in advertisements and on social media.

Filtering, which refers to the process of using software or apps to change the appearance of images posted online. It involves applying digital adjustments like colour changes, texture changes and special effects to make images more visually appealing or to conform to certain standards. Social media platforms offer various filters that users can easily apply to images.

73

While image editing can be a fun way to enhance pictures, it can also have negative effects. Airbrushed and filtered images often create an unrealistic and idealised version of beauty, making people feel insecure about their own bodies and appearance. This can lead to low self-esteem, negative body image and a distorted idea of attractiveness.

ACTIVITY 14.1 – THINK

Indicate whether you think the following statements are true or false and give a reason why.

	Statement	True	False	Why?
1	Image editing has no impact on the self-esteem of individuals who view the edited images.		✓	
2	Online image filters can be easily applied to photos with just a few clicks or taps.	✓		
3	Online image editing is always used to promote body positivity and self-acceptance.		✓	
4	Image filtering is mainly used for enhancing photos. It does not have any impact on videos.		✓	
5	The popularity and usage of image filters have increased significantly since the Covid-19 pandemic.	✓		
6	The more time people spend on social media, the more likely they are to experience negative emotional health.	✓		

ACTIVITY 14.2 – WATCH

A. Watch this video about the impact of edited images on body image and answer the questions that follow.

▶ www.educate*plus*.ie/go/edited-images

1. 'Somewhere along the line, I lost the confidence that I originally had … I feel like social media is one of those factors.' Do you agree with Madison? Can you relate to her comment?
2. Madison states that she was constantly comparing herself to other people and trying 'to be like them'. How did this affect her?

B. Read these statistics about how young people see themselves online. Do any of the statistics surprise you? Why?

12 Number of selfies young people take before posting online

43% of young people worry about how attractive they look online

30% of young people said they have felt sad about their appearance after seeing something online

45% of young people have used a filter in the past year to make themselves look better

CHAPTER 14 – THE EFFECTS OF EDITED IMAGES

ACTIVITY 14.3 – DISCUSS

A. In pairs, examine and discuss these images of celebrities. Determine if they have been edited in any way. If you believe they have, identify the edits made.

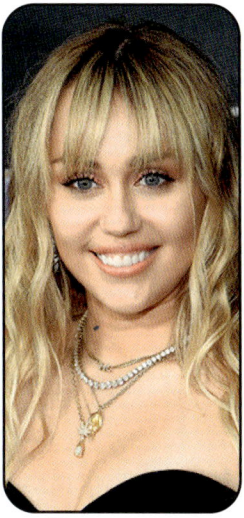

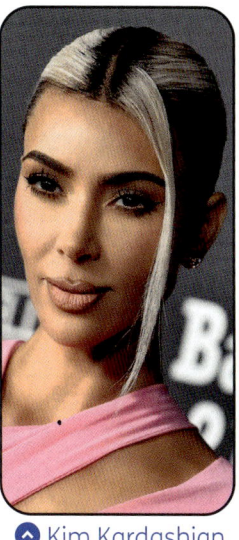

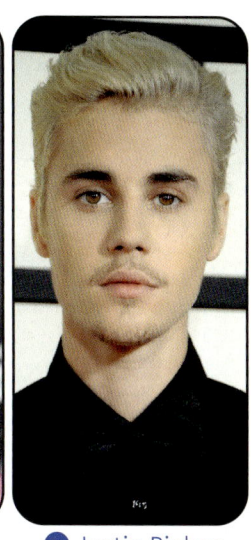

⌃ Beyoncé   ⌃ Zendaya   ⌃ Miley Cyrus   ⌃ Kim Kardashian   ⌃ Justin Bieber

B. Reflection questions:
1. Were you surprised by the extent of airbrushing and filtering that takes place?
2. How has your new awareness of these techniques affected your perception of beauty standards?
3. What negative effects could these edited images have on a person's self-esteem and self-image?
4. How has this activity influenced your perspective on using filters or airbrushing tools? Will you approach them differently in the future?

Here are some tips to help you recognise when images have been edited:

- **Look for unrealistic skin texture:** If the person's skin appears too smooth, flawless or plastic-like, this could be a sign that a skin-smoothing filter or editing tool has been used. Pay attention to areas like the face, where pores and blemishes are more visible.
- **Notice unnatural lighting:** Examine the lighting in the image. If it seems too perfect or is very even throughout, and there are no shadows, this could indicate that the image has been edited.
- **Check for warping:** Look for any warped objects, lines or backgrounds in the image. Strong bending of straight lines can indicate that certain editing tools or filters were used – these tools/filters can unintentionally affect the entire image.
- **Pay attention to unusual body proportions:** Keep an eye out for body proportions that appear unrealistic or distorted, such as an unnaturally tiny waist, long limbs or enlarged body parts.
- **Compare the image:** If you're familiar with the person or their previous images, compare the image to their real-life appearance or other images they've shared. Look for any inconsistencies or drastic differences that may indicate heavy editing.

ACTIVITY 14.4 – WATCH

Watch Beth and Ryan talk about their opinions on posting images online. In pairs, answer the questions that follow.

▶ www.educate*plus*.ie/go/online-body-image-beth

▶ www.educate*plus*.ie/go/online-body-image-ryan

1. Do you agree with any of Beth or Ryan's opinions or experiences? Why?
2. Do you disagree with any of Beth or Ryan's opinions or experiences? Why?
3. Do you think that Beth and Ryan have a healthy relationship with social media? Why?

ACTIVITY 14.5 – READ

In groups, read about and research the following online movements. Explain how they work and present arguments regarding their potential impact on body image, whether positive or negative.

The 'Instagram versus reality' trend

This trend involves sharing an edited image alongside a natural, unedited image. The images are typically accompanied by a caption promoting body positivity and encouraging self-love and self-acceptance. The purpose is to inspire individuals to embrace and love themselves as they are.

The BeReal app

BeReal is a social media app created in 2019. It prompts users to take a photo once a day within a two-minute window, using both the front and back cameras on their phones. The app aims to capture the user and their surroundings authentically, regardless of their location or appearance. By embracing this realness, users can present a more genuine version of themselves online.

CHAPTER 14 – THE EFFECTS OF EDITED IMAGES

Body-positive hashtags

Body-positive hashtags promote self-acceptance, diverse beauty and confidence. They challenge unrealistic standards and celebrate all body types. Popular hashtags include #bodypositivity, #loveyourself and #allbodiesarebeautiful. Hashtags such as #bodyposi, #beyou, #perfectlyimperfect and #confidentyou encourage self-love, while others such as #effyourbeautystandards reject norms.

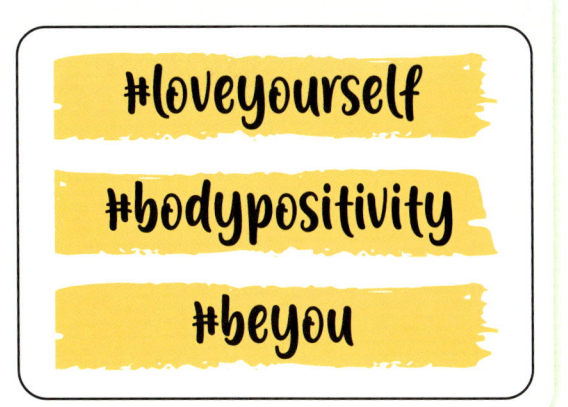

#loveyourself

#bodypositivity

#beyou

ACTIVITY 14.6 – THINK

Personally reflect on the effects of edited images by answering these questions:

1. Do you edit your photos? Why?
2. How do you feel when you use edits?
3. Do you believe image editing affects your self-image, body image or mental health? If so, how?

ACTIVITY 14.7 – THINK

Are you willing to try a social media challenge? Attempt to do the following three things over the next week:

1. Avoid using any filters or edited photos on your social media posts for the entire week. During the week, capture and document your experiences.
2. Scroll through your social media feed and unfollow anyone who makes you feel bad about your body image.
3. Follow people who support real bodies and unedited posts. These are influencers who will make you feel good about your body!

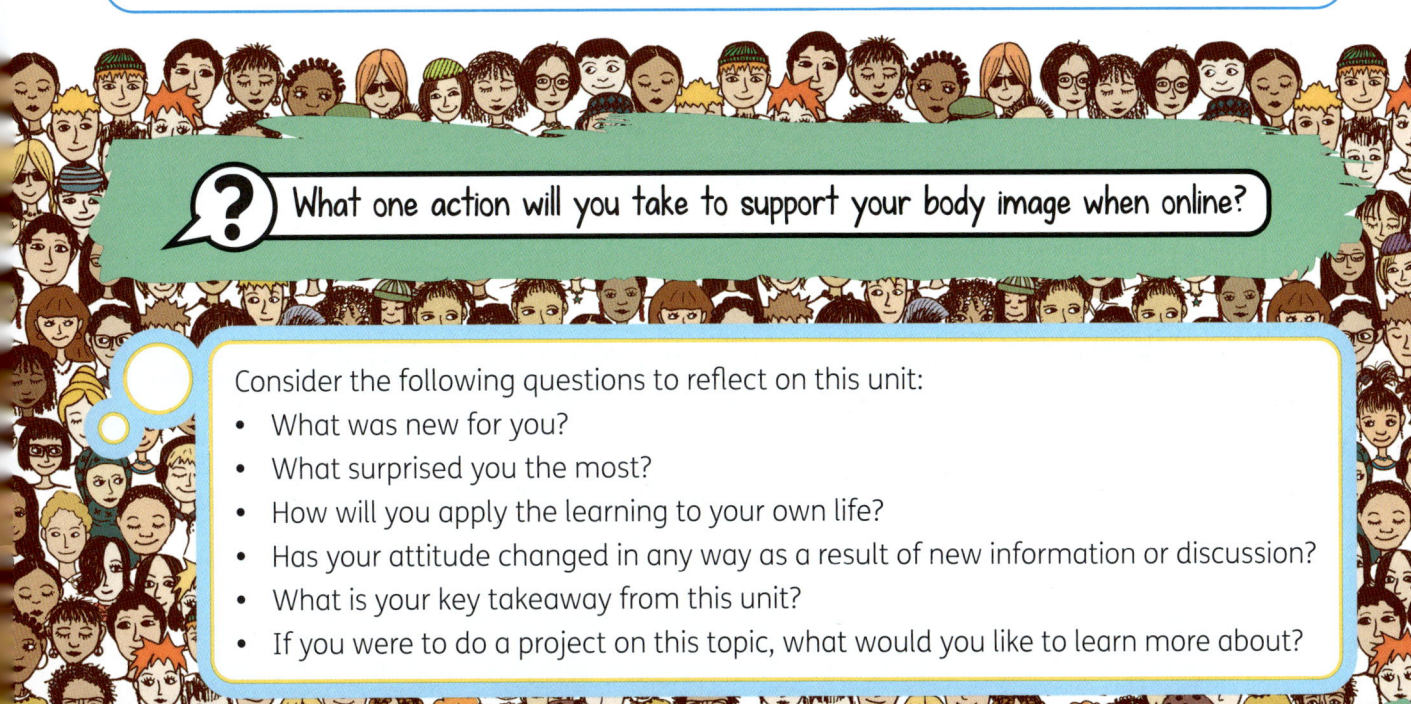

? What one action will you take to support your body image when online?

Consider the following questions to reflect on this unit:
- What was new for you?
- What surprised you the most?
- How will you apply the learning to your own life?
- Has your attitude changed in any way as a result of new information or discussion?
- What is your key takeaway from this unit?
- If you were to do a project on this topic, what would you like to learn more about?

UNIT OF LEARNING 3

Understanding and Dealing with Substance Use

The chapters in this Unit of Learning are:
- Chapter 15 – Problematic Substance Use
- Chapter 16 – Addiction
- Chapter 17 – Substance Use: What Influences Our Choices?
- Chapter 18 – Substance Use and Peer Pressure
- Chapter 19 – Positive Coping Strategies

Note for teachers: This Unit of Learning engages with the following Learning Outcomes:

- **2.3** discuss societal, cultural and economic influences affecting young people when it comes to making healthy choices about smoking, alcohol and other addictive substances and behaviours, and how harmful influences can be overcome in real-life situations
- **2.4** demonstrate skills and strategies to help make informed choices that support health and wellbeing and apply them in real-life situations that may be stressful and/or involve difficult peer situations
- **2.5** discuss the physical, social, emotional and legal consequences of using addictive substances – immediate and long-term
- **2.6** consider scenarios where, for example, alcohol, nicotine, drugs, food and electronic devices might be used to cope with unpleasant feelings or stress, and discuss possible healthy ways of coping
- **2.10** demonstrate how to access and appraise appropriate and trustworthy information, supports and services about health and wellbeing
- **4.5** explore how emotional wellbeing can be affected by factors within our control, such as sleep, diet, exercise, substance use and online exposure, and factors beyond our control

Related Learning Outcomes: 2.5, 4.5.

CHAPTER 15

Problematic Substance Use

In this chapter we will:
- analyse statistics and facts about problematic substance use in Ireland
- discuss binge drinking and the many consequences associated with it
- take a quiz to remind ourselves of the legal consequences of substance use.

KEY TERMS
Binge drinking
Blackouts
Alcohol poisoning

? Identify two negative consequences of abusing alcohol or drugs.

Alcohol and drug use in Ireland

Here are some statistics and facts about alcohol and drug use in Ireland, based on recent surveys and reports:

Alcohol is one of the most prevalent recreational drugs in Ireland and is a major cause of **illness and death** for Irish people.

Alcohol use typically begins in the **teenage years**. During this time, harmful patterns of alcohol consumption may emerge and become established.

One in five drinkers have an alcohol use disorder. This increases to one in three among drinkers aged 15–24 years. Drinkers with an alcohol use disorder are **13 times more likely** to experience alcohol-related harm compared to low-risk drinkers.

While **smoking** rates among adults have reduced, nearly **one quarter** of adults in Ireland report regular heavy alcohol consumption.

One in fourteen people (**seven per cent**) used an illegal drug in the past year.

15–24-year-olds are most likely to report drug use. **Men are twice as likely** as women to use drugs.

Cocaine use has increased across all age groups. **Men aged 25–34** are most likely to report cocaine use.

There is an **increase** in the number of people using illegal stimulants (cocaine, ecstasy, amphetamines) and a **small decrease** in the number of people using illegal cannabis.

ACTIVITY 15.1 – DISCUSS

What signs might there be that someone needs support with their substance use? In pairs, discuss and respond to this question. Consider the following in your discussion:
- How often is the person using a substance?
- How much money are they spending on it?
- Are their relationships with others changing because of substance use?

Binge drinking

Binge drinking involves drinking a large amount of alcohol in a short space of time to get drunk quickly. A report from the World Health Organization (WHO) revealed that Ireland has the second-highest rate of binge drinking in the world. Another report found that 39 per cent of all Irish people aged 15 and over had engaged in binge drinking in the past month. Rates of binge drinking are more than twice as high for men than women.

Many people engage in binge drinking to:
- escape their problems
- fit in with friends
- enjoy themselves during a night out
- experience a sense of relaxation.

However, binge drinking is very problematic and has many consequences:

Short-term consequences	Long-term consequences
• Vomiting • Loss of control • Loss of consciousness • Drink driving • Exposure to violence or engagement in violent acts • Unsafe sex • **Blackouts**: A temporary memory loss that occurs while drinking	• Physical and mental dependence on alcohol • Liver and brain damage • Increased risk of cancers of the throat, mouth and oesophagus • Increased likelihood of developing mental health problems, such as depression and anxiety • Existing mental health problems are intensified

A major potential consequence of binge drinking is **alcohol poisoning**, which is a severe and possibly life-threatening condition. When someone experiences alcohol poisoning, their body is unable to process the alcohol efficiently, leading to a dangerous build-up of alcohol in the bloodstream. This can have serious effects on the central nervous system, respiratory system and other vital functions within the body.

Symptoms and consequences of alcohol poisoning may include:

- confusion
- vomiting
- seizures
- slow or irregular breathing
- blue-tinged or pale skin
- low body temperature
- unconsciousness
- coma
- death, in severe cases.

Alcohol poisoning is a medical emergency, and professional medical care is needed to prevent severe complications or death. If you suspect someone has alcohol poisoning, seek immediate medical attention by dialling 999 or 112. Turn the person on their side and place a cushion under their head. Do not leave them alone.

ACTIVITY 15.2 – THINK

'Binge drinking is okay as long as you don't do it too often.' Do you agree or disagree with this statement? Your teacher will designate one end of the classroom as 'Agree', the other end as 'Disagree' and the middle of the classroom as 'Unsure'. When asked, walk to the part of the room that reflects your answer.

ACTIVITY 15.3 – THINK

There can also be legal consequences of substance use. Take this 'true or false' quiz to test your knowledge about substance use and the law in Ireland.

	Statement	True	False
1	It is illegal for anyone under 18 to buy alcohol in a shop or buy a drink in a pub.		
2	If you are 18 or over, it is illegal to buy alcohol for anyone under 18. The penalty is a maximum fine of €500.		
3	It is illegal to pretend to be over 18 to obtain alcohol.		
4	The Gardaí can take alcohol off under 18s who are drinking in a public place. They can also contact their parents.		
5	Young people under the age of 15 are allowed into a bar at any time.		
6	If you are over 18, a bar owner can legally serve you alcoholic drinks if you are drunk.		
7	Under Irish law, it is considered an offence to be in possession of a controlled drug and this means that you could receive a fine or a prison sentence of up to 12 months.		
8	Cannabis in Ireland is legal for recreational purposes.		

ACTIVITY 15.4 – READ

In groups, read these three case studies and answer the questions that follow.

Case study 1

Michael drank too much at a party the other night and embarrassed himself by flirting with everyone in the room. He also threw up all over a couch on which people were sitting.

1. Are there consequences (physical, social, emotional, legal) to Michael's excessive drinking at the party?
2. What, in your opinion, is the biggest concern for Michael?
3. What lessons can Michael learn from the situation?

Case study 2

Bronagh's friend buys some ecstasy tablets and gives her a few. Bronagh decides she might take some on Friday night before the disco, and then sell the rest to one or two girls she knows. She wants to buy a new phone, so the money would come in really handy.

1. Will there be consequences (physical, social, emotional, legal) to Bronagh's decision?
2. What, in your opinion, is the biggest concern for Bronagh?
3. What advice would you give Bronagh if you were her friend?

Case study 3

While celebrating her 16th birthday, Jasmine drank too much and passed out. She didn't wake up for hours, and she couldn't remember much of what happened during the party.

1. Are there consequences (physical, social, emotional, legal) to Jasmine's excessive drinking and blackout?
2. What, in your opinion, is the biggest concern for Jasmine?
3. What lessons can Jasmine learn from the situation?

? In your opinion, what is the most serious consequence of binge drinking?

Related Learning Outcomes: 2.3, 2.5, 2.10.

CHAPTER 16

Addiction

In this chapter we will:
- explain what addiction is and how it can affect individuals
- explore addictive behaviours and their consequences
- examine the four stages of substance addiction
- identify sources of support and ways to seek help for substance use and addiction.

KEY TERMS
Addiction
Addictive behaviour
Withdrawal symptoms

? What is an addictive substance? Can you give an example of one?

What is addiction?

Addiction is the repeated use of a substance despite the harm it causes to one's health and wellbeing. It can also refer to a lack of control over engaging in or using something. While addiction is frequently linked to gambling, drugs, alcohol and smoking, people can also become addicted to other substances and activities. Addiction can also be referred to as a substance use disorder.

ACTIVITY 16.1 – THINK
Can you think of other things in life, apart from gambling, drugs, smoking and alcohol, that people commonly become addicted to? As a class, brainstorm and make a list of these addictions.

> **ACTIVITY 16.2 – WATCH**
>
> In pairs, watch this video about drug addiction and the brain and answer the questions that follow.
>
> ▶ www.educateplus.ie/go/addiction-and-brain
>
> 1. What is addiction also known as?
> 2. How many people will experience addiction at some point in their lives?
> 3. Which two parts of the brain are affected by drug use?
> 4. What factors contribute to the development of a substance use disorder?
> 5. What key factors aid in preventing addiction?
> 6. At what age do those with substance use disorders commonly first use the substance?
> 7. Is addiction treatable? How?

Addictive behaviours

People who are addicted to something display addictive behaviours. An **addictive behaviour** is an intense focus on a particular activity, substance or object, to the exclusion of other things or activities in a person's life. The behaviour constantly occupies the person's thoughts and starts to cause physical, mental or social harm to them or those around them.

Despite experiencing negative consequences such as physical symptoms, poor performance in work or studies and difficult relationships with others, the person persistently (continuously) engages in the behaviour and struggles to quit doing it. They can also deny any problems that arise from their behaviour, and be secretive about it around family and friends.

People with addictive behaviours:

- often have low self-esteem and anxiety when they lack control over their surroundings
- frequently come from backgrounds of mental or physical abuse
- can experience depression, which shows the importance of seeking medical help to understand the underlying causes of the behaviour.

If a person stops engaging in addictive behaviours and gives up the activity, substance or object they are addicted to, they often experience **withdrawal symptoms**, which are unpleasant physical or mental side effects:

Physical	Mental
• Sweating • Heart palpitations (pounding heart) • Headaches • Tightness in the chest • Tremors (parts of the body shaking) • Nausea • Vomiting • Diarrhoea	• Irritability • Cravings • Restlessness • Depression • Anxiety • Poor concentration • Feeling 'low' • Insomnia (inability to fall asleep)

ACTIVITY 16.3 – READ

Despite their fame and fortune, many celebrities have suffered from an addiction to drugs or alcohol. This shows that addiction is possible no matter who you are.

In groups, read this case study about Daniel Radcliffe's experience of addiction and answer the questions that follow.

Case study: Daniel Radcliffe

Daniel Radcliffe was just 11 years old when the first Harry Potter movie made him a huge movie star. As the film series progressed, he remained very much in the public eye, and viewers watched him grow up. He finished filming the final movie, *Harry Potter and the Deathly Hallows: Part 2*, just before reaching the age of 22. The enormous pressure of playing a universally loved character was not easy to deal with. During the filming of the later movies in the series, Daniel developed a significant dependence on alcohol.

Daniel has spoken about the sense of being watched by the public and the media in his late teenage years, and how this feeling contributed to an ongoing cycle of alcohol addiction: 'The quickest way of forgetting about the fact that you were being watched was to get very drunk. And then as you get very drunk, you become aware that "oh, people are watching more now because I'm getting very drunk, so I should probably drink more to ignore that more."'

Daniel began to realise that the amount he was drinking was making him unhappy. He recalls how he used to black out when drinking and wouldn't remember what had happened. He would fall asleep and wake up in the morning to texts from friends, asking if he was okay. It worried him that he felt unable to look after himself when he drank too much – he felt like a burden to his friends.

Daniel is very grateful to the people in his personal and professional life for giving him support, guidance and good advice. However, he ultimately had to decide to quit drinking himself. Daniel is open and honest about his past struggles with alcohol addiction and now lives his life without consuming alcohol.

1. What contributed to Daniel's alcohol addiction?
2. What helped Daniel to recover?
3. Daniel is very open about his addiction issues. What do you think of this?
4. 'There is a dark side to fame.' Do you agree with this common statement?
5. Why, in your opinion, do so many celebrities suffer or have suffered from addiction?

The four stages of substance addiction

Stage 1: Experimentation

Addiction often starts out as experimentation. Teenagers might experiment with substances like drugs and alcohol because of peer pressure or curiosity. This also applies to adults. Other reasons for experimentation may include:
- managing stress
- reducing social anxiety
- dealing with difficult life situations
- relieving physical discomfort.

Some people might experiment and leave it at that. However, for other people, this first stage could open the door to the next stage of addiction.

Stage 2: Regular use

In this stage, substance use may become a lifestyle rather than a temporary or recreational thing. As a person uses substances more regularly, they may find that what once helped relieve stress or boredom is now one of the factors contributing to it. Regular use can increase the risk of:
- severe mood swings
- depression and anxiety
- preoccupation with substances
- withdrawal from friends and family
- lack of interest in activities once enjoyed
- risky behaviours, such as driving under the influence of drugs or alcohol.

Stage 3: Dependency

After repeated substance use, a person builds a tolerance to the substance. They now start to crave and rely on it more and more, to the point where they prioritise substance use over other things in life. Signs of this stage may include:
- physical or mental cravings
- depression
- irritability
- tiredness.

Some behavioural changes commonly seen in this stage include:
- needing stronger, more frequent doses
- borrowing or stealing money
- missing days of school or college, allowing academic results to slip
- neglecting family, friends or work
- changing peer groups.

Stage 4: Addiction

When fully addicted, substance users often spend most of their time thinking about how to get their next high. At this point, they may not be able to quit without help, even if they want to. Some behavioural changes commonly seen in this stage include:
- skipping meals
- neglecting basic needs
- lacking personal hygiene and an interest in their appearance
- lacking sleep
- having no daily routine
- experiencing suicidal thoughts.

Consequences of this stage might include:
- job loss
- increase in criminal behaviour
- poverty
- seeking charity
- low immunity, leading to infections and diseases.

Where can we seek support?

While addiction is very serious, there are many sources of support for people. Early intervention is key, so the sooner a person seeks help, the better it will be for them, their family and their friends. Some supports are listed below.

Family members or friends
Family members or friends could offer emotional support and guidance, and help the person access additional support services.

GP
A person's GP can provide confidential medical advice and may refer them for treatment or prescribe treatment options.

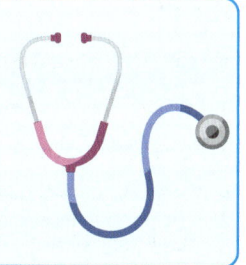

Teachers
Teachers are available for students to raise any concerns or ask questions about substances. They can listen to worries and direct students to further supports within the school (counsellor, student support team, designated liaison person, etc.) or external support services (Bodywhys, the HSE drugs helpline, etc.).

Childline
Childline is a service available to young people up to and including the age of 18. A young person can speak with Childline's 24-hour support line in confidence, about anything that might be on their mind, without judgement. They do not give out or tell people what to do.

Childline can be contacted by phone for free at 1800 66 66 66, at any time of day or night. There is also a live chat option on their website, accessible via the 'Live Chat' button. See **www.childline.ie**

HSE Drugs and Alcohol Helpline
The HSE Drugs and Alcohol Helpline provides support, information, guidance and referral to anyone with a question or concern related to drug and alcohol use. The service is non-judgemental and offers space to talk about a person's situation, consider their needs and explore some options. During contact, staff refer to a database of over 400 services nationwide.

This confidential service has both a freephone helpline (1800 459 459) and an email support service (**helpline@hse.ie**). See **www.educateplus.ie/go/hse-services**

ACTIVITY 16.4 – READ

In groups, read the scenarios on the next page and decide on the advice that you would give to these young people. Write an email to one of the young people outlining your advice to them. Consider the following questions in your discussion:
- In each scenario, what signs might there be that someone needs support with their substance use?
- What stage of addiction do you think they are at?
- How can this person be helped to break the addiction?
- Where could they seek additional support?

Scenario 1: Rory

I have been smoking for a few years now, but I've recently been thinking about quitting. The problem is, I have no idea where to start! My friends smoke so it's difficult to avoid it, and I don't think that they'll really help or encourage me.

Scenario 2: Sorcha

I'm worried about my friend Cathy, who has started taking drugs recently. She's been hanging out with some new people and I think they've pressured her into smoking weed. I'm not sure she even enjoys it very much!

Scenario 3: Brian

My dad passed away recently and my brother hasn't taken it very well. He won't talk about anything, and he spends a lot of time alone in his room or out with his friends until late. I know he has been taking some tablets – I saw them in his bedroom. But I don't know if I should tell anyone.

Scenario 4: Zaneta

My parents have always enjoyed having a few drinks, but recently I've noticed that my dad has been drinking a lot more. He seems to start drinking earlier and earlier in the day, and now when I get home from school, he's usually already drunk. Last night he got into a temper and pushed my mum.

ACTIVITY 16.5 – CREATE

In groups, create an awareness campaign about drug addiction, using information from reliable sources. In your campaign, include the following:

- A poster or infographic highlighting the main points of your campaign. Decide on a unique hashtag for your campaign.
- A digital presentation or video containing information about the symptoms, stages and effects of drug addiction.
- A short pamphlet containing resources that help people overcome addiction, such as websites, helpline numbers and local support groups.

> **?** State one thing that you have learned about addiction in this chapter. Name one person or service that someone with addiction issues could contact for support.

Related Learning Outcome: 2.3.

CHAPTER 17

Substance Use: What Influences Our Choices?

In this chapter we will:
- identify the different types of influences that affect our decision making
- discuss how external pressures can affect substance use
- explore how to overcome harmful influences
- evaluate potential barriers and benefits to seeking support
- explain how to seek help for issues with substance use.

KEY TERMS
Societal influence
Cultural influence
Economic influence
Socio-economic influence

? Identify three factors that can influence our choices in life.

What influences us

There are many influences that affect our decisions and behaviours. These influences can be positive or negative. Negative influences can lead us to do things that are harmful to our health and wellbeing, both in the short term and the long term. Understanding how we are influenced helps us to make more rational decisions and have more control over our lives.

Here are some of the influences that affect our decision making:

1. Societal influence

Societal influence refers to the ways in which we are influenced by the people around us, our communities and the societies we live in. Peer pressure is one of the most common examples of societal influence, as people may act in a certain way to be accepted or to fit in.

Societal influences can cause people to smoke, drink, vape or use drugs in order to gain others' approval. Societal factors such as the number of off licences, pubs or drug dealers in an area can also influence people's choices around substance use. The closeness of these factors to schools or recreational areas can particularly expose young people to substances.

2. Cultural influence

Cultural influence refers to the ways in which we are influenced by the shared beliefs, values, traditions and customs of our racial, religious or social groups. These factors can play a significant role in shaping young people's choices around addictive substances or behaviours. They can either support or hinder healthy decision making.

3. Economic influence

Economic influence refers to the ways in which we are influenced by economic factors such as the availability, affordability and marketing of goods and services. These economic factors can affect young people's choices around using addictive substances:

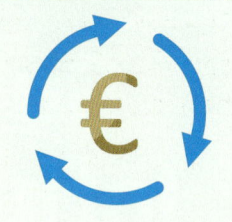

- **Availability:** When something is readily available and easily accessible, there is a greater temptation to try it. For example, young people may obtain substances from their friends and peers.
- **Affordability:** Lower prices can make substances more appealing and increase the likelihood of experimentation or regular use.
- **Marketing:** Companies that produce nicotine and alcohol products heavily invest in advertising campaigns to sell their products. In these campaigns, the products are often associated with fun, excitement and social acceptance. Young people are particularly vulnerable to these messages.

4. Socio-economic influence

Socio-economic influence refers to the ways in which we are influenced by a mixture of societal and economic factors. Factors such as poverty, unemployment and a lack of educational opportunities can contribute to substance use.

Young people facing socio-economic challenges may experience stress, lack support structures and have limited access to resources, which can increase the likelihood of engaging in risky behaviours.

Overcoming harmful influences requires a combination of personal resilience, a supportive environment and effective educational strategies.

ACTIVITY 17.1 – READ

In pairs, read these three case studies and answer the questions that follow.

Case study 1

John is working his first part-time job at his neighbour's supermarket. It's time for the annual Christmas party, and most of John's colleagues are going. However, John's neighbour can't make it. John is happy about this – he can socialise and have fun at the party without his neighbour watching over him.

CHAPTER 17 – SUBSTANCE USE: WHAT INFLUENCES OUR CHOICES?

At the party, everyone takes turns buying a round of drinks. John quickly feels quite intoxicated, but he keeps accepting drinks because he wants to fit in with his colleagues. Before he knows it, it's midnight and he has lost track of how much alcohol he has consumed. Being very drunk, he begins telling his colleagues stories about his neighbour. Everyone finds the stories hilarious, and this encourages John to keep going.

The next day, John barely remembers what he had said at the party. However, he overhears some of his colleagues telling one of his stories, and he realises that his neighbour might have heard it too.

1. What might John be thinking and feeling when he decides to accept drinks and tell stories to his colleagues?
2. How might John's behaviour be influenced by where he is, or by the people around him? Are there any external pressures that John might be experiencing?
3. How do you think John feels after the party? How might it affect him the next day?

Case study 2

Dervla has been at university for a few months. She has joined one of the university's sports teams, which is known for having big parties during the week. These parties are really popular and, as a result, the team is well liked around campus. However, Dervla knows that the team has been in trouble with the university in the past, and that some people have complained about the behaviour of certain members.

As a member of the team, she is invited to all the parties. Whenever she attends, she is offered alcohol and some other substances that everyone seems to be taking. When she takes them, she begins to relax but then feels quite ill the next morning.

Although Dervla likes being invited to the parties, she is beginning to notice that they're having an impact on the rest of her life.

1. What might Dervla be thinking and feeling when she decides to drink and take other substances at the parties?
2. How might Dervla's behaviour be influenced by where she is, or by the people around her? Are there any external pressures that Dervla might be experiencing?
3. What negative effects do you think these parties are having on Dervla?
4. Are there any short-term or long-term consequences that Dervla might face as a result of her behaviour?

Case study 3

Sean is from a large city. He would describe the area he lives in as very rough. A lot of anti-social behaviour occurs there, along with crimes such as car robberies, vandalism and violent fights. Sean started to inject heroin at a very young age and believes that he was influenced by all that was going on around him, as well as the many addicts and dealers in the area. He thinks that things could have been different if he had grown up elsewhere.

1. What might Sean be thinking and feeling about his circumstances and drug use?
2. How might Sean's behaviour be influenced by where he is, or by the people around him? Are there any external pressures that Sean might be experiencing?
3. What are the consequences for Sean?

Overcoming harmful influences

Here are eight strategies that can help young people overcome harmful influences:

1. Family and friends
The values and attitudes of family members and friends greatly impact a young person's choices. When a person's social circle promotes healthy behaviours and discourages substance abuse, this can act as a protective factor.

2. Education
Education that provides accurate information about the risks and consequences of substance abuse can empower young people to make informed decisions.

3. Community engagement
Community initiatives, such as after-school programmes, sports clubs and youth organisations, provide young people with positive role models and alternative activities. Engaging in these activities can help prevent boredom and reduce the likelihood of turning to harmful substances.

4. Building resilience
Building resilience and developing coping skills is crucial. This includes learning to manage stress, making assertive decisions, resisting peer pressure and seeking support when needed. Resilience helps young people to avoid negative influences and make healthier choices.

5. Media and advertising

Media and advertising can be very influential on young people, especially when it comes to substance use. The media can help reduce the influence of harmful messages by:
- portraying positive healthy behaviours
- restricting nicotine and alcohol advertising that targets young people
- promoting campaigns that do not glamorise substance use
- providing accurate information about the short-term and long-term consequences of substance use.

6. Supportive relationships

Nurturing positive relationships with trusted adults, such as parents, teachers or counsellors, creates a supportive environment. They can provide guidance, encouragement and a safe space to discuss concerns or challenges related to substance abuse. Young people should also seek support from trusted adults when faced with economic influences that may compromise their health and wellbeing.

7. Peer support and peer pressure resistance

It's important for young people to gain peer support and interact with like-minded individuals who prioritise healthy choices. It's crucial for young people to develop strong communication skills and assertiveness. This includes setting personal boundaries and practising saying 'no'.

8. Financial supports

Governments can increase taxation on addictive substances and allocate resources to prevention programmes and interventions. Making these substances less affordable and less readily available makes it more challenging for young people to engage in unhealthy behaviours.

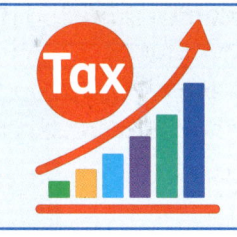

ACTIVITY 17.2 – DISCUSS

A. In pairs, discuss the eight strategies for overcoming harmful influences. There will be posters of the strategies on the wall of the classroom. Decide which strategy you think would work best and explain why. Place a green mark on the poster of this strategy. Then decide which strategy you think would be the most difficult to successfully undertake. Place a red mark on the poster of this strategy.

Family and friends	Education	Community engagement	Building resilience	Media and advertising	Supportive relationships	Peer support and peer pressure resistance	Financial supports
•• •	••	••• •	• •	•• ••	•• •	• ••	•• ••• •

B. Reflection questions:
1. Can you think of any other strategies for overcoming harmful influences?
2. Which strategy would you try if you were being influenced to make an unhealthy choice?

Seeking support

Harmful influences may affect our choices around substance use, but help is always available to overcome them. Seeking support isn't always easy – there may be barriers that prevent us from doing so. However, it's important to seek support as soon as possible to reduce the risks associated with substance use. See Chapter 16 (page 87) for a list of the supports and services available.

ACTIVITY 17.3 – THINK

In groups, brainstorm answers to the questions below. Consider the experiences of John, Dervla and Sean from Activity 17.1 in your discussion.

1. What barriers or challenges might someone face when seeking support for concerns relating to substance use?

2. What might be the benefits of seeking support for concerns relating to substance use?

ACTIVITY 17.4 – THINK

In pairs, review the list of supports on page 87. Consider the experiences of John, Dervla and Sean from Activity 17.1 and note down who they could turn to for support if they made the decision to do so.

	Source of support
John	
Dervla	
Sean	

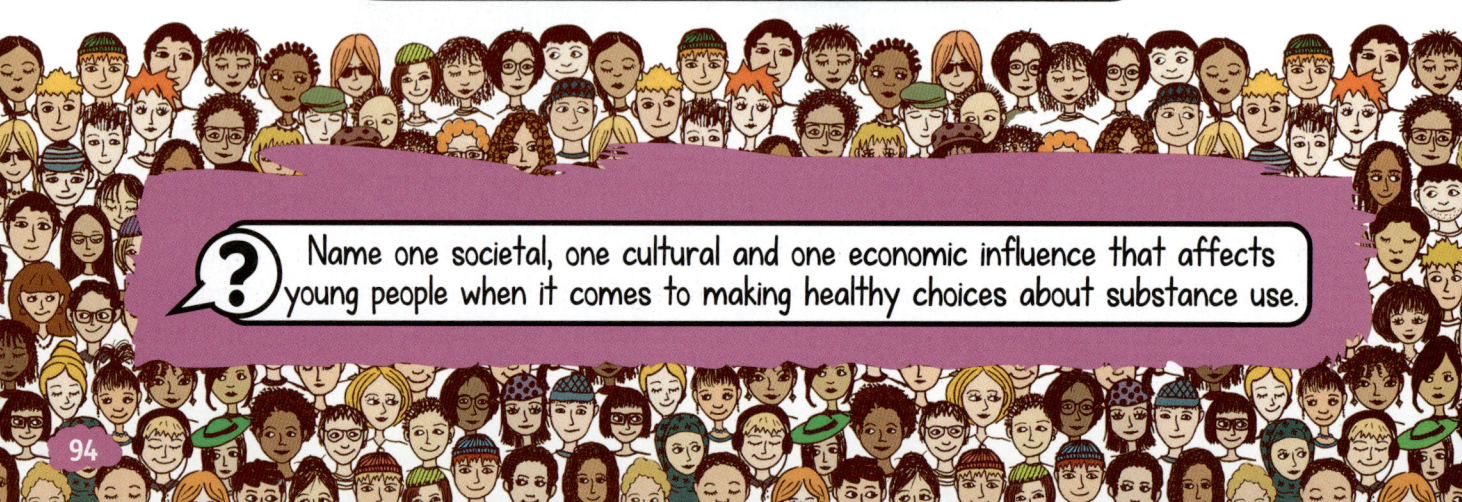

? Name one societal, one cultural and one economic influence that affects young people when it comes to making healthy choices about substance use.

Related Learning Outcome: 2.4.

CHAPTER 18

Substance Use and Peer Pressure

In this chapter we will:
- ✓ examine peer pressure as an influencing factor
- ✓ evaluate whether peer pressure influences our decisions
- ✓ explore ways to resist peer pressure
- ✓ practise skills to deal with peer pressure and substance use.

KEY TERMS
Peer pressure

? Can you identify two ways people can cope with peer pressure?

Peer pressure as an influencing factor

Our decisions and actions are influenced by various internal and external factors, such as:
- personal needs
- beliefs
- values
- family relationships
- friendships
- media exposure
- community environment
- legal regulations.

These factors can have both positive and negative effects:

Positive
They can provide valuable guidance, help us clarify our thoughts, and enable us to learn new skills. For example, our friends can offer us good advice in difficult situations.

Negative
When certain factors play a big a role in our decisions and actions, this can be damaging. For example, persuasive advertisements can prompt unnecessary purchases.

It's important for us to reflect on how we might behave in different situations, and to recognise the factors that shape our behaviour. By developing a heightened awareness and understanding of the different influences in our lives, we can make informed choices that support our health and wellbeing more effectively.

One powerful influencing factor on young people is **peer pressure**, which is the strong influence of a group of people on members of that same group to act or behave in a certain way. People tend to be more strongly influenced by their close friends, and the impact of peer pressure reaches its peak around the ages of 15 to 16 before beginning to decline. Most young people first use substances (legal and illegal) with their friends. This is often determined by how prevalent (common) substance use is within the peer group.

Peer pressure can sometimes make it difficult for us to be independent, but fortunately, we can develop skills to resist it.

ACTIVITY 18.1 – DISCUSS

In pairs, brainstorm examples of peer pressure. For example: making a person feel bad about not doing something, so that they will eventually do it.

The examples can be imaginary and don't need to be from your own personal experience. Think about what peer pressure affects: what you choose to wear, the TV programmes you watch, etc.

Write your ideas on a Post-it note and hand it to your teacher.

ACTIVITY 18.2 – THINK

A. Does peer pressure influence your decision making? Take this quiz to evaluate how good you are at making decisions. In each scenario, indicate which decision you would make. Then analyse your results.

Scenario 1		You would:	
You've studied really hard for your History test tomorrow, and you're ready to do it. Two very popular girls are seated on either side of you in History class, and they both want you to let them copy off your paper.	A	Let them copy in the hope they'll become your friends and help you seem really cool at school.	○
	B	Stay at home and pretend to be sick.	○
	C	Tell them that cheating is wrong, and you don't want to be involved.	○

Scenario 2		You would:	
A very popular student in Transition Year has just asked you out to a party, and your friends think you should go because it will help you break into the 'in' crowd. However, you've sometimes seen this student making fun of other students around school, and you know that this is not okay.	A	Say 'no thanks' and risk becoming the next student who gets picked on.	○
	B	Say your parents have grounded you from leaving the house and hope the student loses interest.	○
	C	Say 'yes' in order to gain popularity, and try to ignore the fact that this student often does and says mean things to others.	○

Scenario 3		You would:	
Someone has brought alcohol to the disco, and you've just caught some of your friends getting drunk. They want you to 'relax and start enjoying yourself' by drinking with them.	A	Have a couple of sips just to make it look like you're part of the group.	○
	B	Give in and get drunk so your friends don't think you're lame.	○
	C	Tell your friends that you're already enjoying yourself and don't want to drink.	○

CHAPTER 18 – SUBSTANCE USE AND PEER PRESSURE

| Scenario 4
You and your friends really want to go to the cinema, but none of you have enough money to get in. One friend suggests sneaking in through the exit door. Some of the group think this sounds like a good idea, and they want you to come along.		You would:	
	A	Decide to give it a try to stop your friends from thinking you're a coward.	○
	B	Tell your friends that you're going home to try to get more money, and then just not return.	○
	C	Suggest to your friends that it would be better to watch a movie on Netflix at home.	○
Scenario 5
Your older brother was supposed to give you and three of your friends a lift to the shopping centre, but he cancelled at the last minute. The shopping centre is over 5 km away, and one of your friends suggests hitchhiking. Everyone else is willing to do it, but you know it might not be safe.		You would:	
	A	Make up an excuse to leave, such as you just remembered you promised to help your parents with a task.	○
	B	Remind your friends that there are plenty of people who went missing while hitchhiking, and tell them you'd rather wait until you can get a lift from someone you know.	○
	C	Give in because you don't want to be left behind.	○

RESULTS:

Scenario 1
The best decision is C. The others are not good decisions. People who just want to use you will never be true friends. You should also not feel like you have to lie in any situation.

Scenario 2
The best decision is A. The others are not good decisions. Deciding to go out with this student, or lying to try to avoid them, can leave you feeling guilty, uncomfortable and stressed.

Scenario 3
The best decision is C. The others are not good decisions. You would be risking your own health and safety, and through your participation also encouraging your friends to do the same.

Scenario 4
The best decision is C. The others are not good decisions. A good friend wouldn't pressure you to break the law. Going home is one way to exit the situation, but doing so here means that you still felt too pressured to confront your friends.

Scenario 5
The best decision is B. The others are not good decisions. You should never take part in any activity that could put your life at risk. While option A would help you get out of a potentially dangerous situation, keep in mind that it was your friends' pressure that caused you to make up an excuse to leave.

B. Reflection questions:
1. How many good decisions did you make?
2. How good are your decisions?
3. Do you feel that you tend to be a 'people pleaser'?
4. Do you feel too embarrassed to say 'no' to your friends?
5. Is it easier to just give in?
6. Do you feel like you should do what people expect of you?
7. What are the consequences, for you and others, of giving in to peer pressure?

Resisting peer pressure

You should never feel pressured to say 'yes' when you want to say 'no'. Having the ability to say 'no', and mean it, can get you out of uncomfortable or difficult situations. It might even save your life. However, saying 'no' is not always easy. You might feel like your friendships or peer relationships would suffer.

If you worry about resisting peer pressure, or feel unsure about how to do it, here is some advice:

Say 'no' and mean it

No should always mean no. It's not up for negotiation, and a person should respect your decision. State your position clearly in a firm but non-confrontational way. For example: 'No, thanks. I'm not into it.'

Avoid apologising too much or trying to justify yourself. You can explain your reasoning if you wish, but you shouldn't feel pressured to answer for your decision.

If the other person is being persistent, politely ask them to stop. If this doesn't work, walk away and avoid further conversation. If the person is putting pressure on you, or is in danger of putting themselves or others at risk, you may need to inform an adult.

Be mindful of body language

Saying 'no' while smiling or fidgeting could send mixed messages. 'No' is more clearly communicated through body language when you stand your ground, make eye contact and remain calm. Sometimes, the best strategy is to simply walk away and distance yourself from potential trouble.

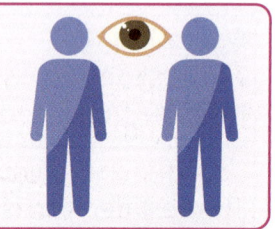

Offer alternatives

You may hesitate to say 'no' because you think it will make you unpopular with your friends. No one wants to be the odd one out, or to seem boring, judgemental or unreliable. If saying 'no' outright is too difficult, a helpful strategy is to offer alternatives. For example, if you were feeling peer pressured by your friend to skip class, you could respond with: 'I'm going to class, but I'll meet up with you straight after school.'

Express your values

When you make a choice that is right for you and stick with it, you learn to express your values. Remember that you are your own person making your own choices. It's up to you, not your friends or peers, to decide what you value. For example, if you value safety, you would not agree to walk home in a dangerous area late at night.

Reconsider your friendships

Remember that you have the right to refuse a request. This doesn't mean that you dislike the person. It simply means that you don't wish to take part in a particular activity.

If your friends persistently pressure you to do things, then perhaps you should start thinking about finding a new group of friends. A true friend will always respect you and your decisions.

CHAPTER 18 – SUBSTANCE USE AND PEER PRESSURE

ACTIVITY 18.3 – ROLE PLAY

A. Practice makes perfect! Here you will have the opportunity to practise strategies to resist peer pressure.

Your teacher will separate the class into groups of three. Each group will script and act out one of the following five role plays. In the role play, Character A needs to refuse the request assertively. Within your group, take turns playing Character A, Character B and an Observer. The role of the Observer is to observe, give feedback and offer suggestions on how to be more assertive.

Role play 1

You (Character A) have moved to a new area and are at a camogie match with a new friend. Your friend (Character B) offers you an e-cigarette. They have just used one and want you to join in. When you hesitate, your friend starts insisting that you use it.

Role play 2

You (Character A) are babysitting with a friend (Character B) and they suggest drinking some vodka that they found in the kitchen press. You don't want to.

Role play 3

You (Character A) are at a disco and someone you like (Character B) offers you some cannabis. You want to be cool, but you don't really want to start smoking it.

Role play 4

Your team has just won a county final match and you're now in the pub. You (Character A) don't drink and have said 'no' but your friend (Character B) is determined to persuade you. They are really persistent and it's becoming quite annoying.

Role play 5

You (Character A) had been caught smoking by your parents and had been grounded until recently. You're now at a concert and your friend (Character B) offers you a cigarette. You don't want to seem nerdy by refusing, but you also don't want to upset your parents by smoking again.

B. Reflection questions:
1. How did it feel to play the role of Character A? Was it easy to resist the peer pressure?
2. How did it feel to play the role of Character B?
3. How did it feel to be the Observer? What did you notice during the role play?
4. What are your main takeaways from this activity? Did you learn anything new about yourself?

ACTIVITY 18.4 – CREATE

In groups of eight, create a short video clip of you acting out a role play. The theme of the role play is 'substance use and peer pressure'. The role play must show a group of friends pressuring their friends into doing something that makes them feel uncomfortable or unsafe. Follow these steps:

1. Think about a situation involving vaping, smoking, consuming alcohol or taking drugs.
2. Revise the advice for resisting peer pressure.
3. Script a role play of the situation.
4. Decide on the roles each of you will play.
5. Practise the role play aloud.
6. Edit it and make changes, if necessary.
7. Record your role play using a recording device.
8. Watch the recording and write a reflection on how it marked important learning for you in SPHE.

? Why is it important to resist peer pressure when it comes to substance use?

Related Learning Outcome: 2.6.

CHAPTER 19

Positive Coping Strategies

In this chapter we will:
- explore the link between stress and substance use
- discover positive coping strategies
- identify stressors in our lives and ways to deal with them.

KEY TERMS
- Stress
- Stressor
- Traumatic experience

? Identify one negative way and one positive way that someone could cope with a stressor in their life.

The link between stress and substance use

According to research, there is a strong link between a person's exposure to stress and traumatic experiences (especially in childhood) and substance use and abuse:

Stress is a normal reaction that occurs in the body due to changes in a person's environment. It acts as an alarm and can trigger a physical and emotional response. A **stressor** is something that causes stress, such as an upcoming exam or an argument.

A **traumatic experience** is an incident that causes physical, emotional or psychological harm. A person may feel physically threatened or extremely frightened as a result of this experience. Examples include a serious car accident or the death of a family member. Stress is a common response to traumatic events.

Substance use and abuse

101

Everyone copes with stress and stressors in different ways. Some people turn to substances such as alcohol or drugs to deal with stress. However, there is a two-way relationship between stress and substance use:

STRESS → Stress may cause people to turn to substances to help them cope. → **SUBSTANCE USE**

However, substances like alcohol and drugs can also contribute to stress.

Other links between stress and substance use include the following:
- People who experience chronic (long-term) stress and lack effective coping tools may resort to using drugs or alcohol as a way to deal with it. This chronic stress can also be a contributing factor to addiction.
- Negative consequences related to substance use, such as a lack of money, job loss, relationship difficulties or health problems, can significantly increase stress levels.
- If someone attempts to cut back or stop using alcohol or drugs, they may experience withdrawal symptoms. These unpleasant physical or mental side effects can be incredibly stressful. In order to ease these symptoms, the person may return to drug or alcohol use.

ACTIVITY 19.1 – WATCH

A. Watch this video about different types of stressors. In your copy, fill in the table below with an example of each type of stressor.

▶ www.educate*plus*.ie/go/stress-causes

Physical		Environmental	
Chemical		Circumstantial	
Biological		Psychological	
Social			

B. Reflection questions:
1. Which of these stressors would be a source of stress for you?
2. Which stressor would not cause you too much stress?
3. Which type of stressor is the most serious, in your opinion?

Positive coping strategies

Here are some positive coping strategies that can be used instead of substance use to manage stress:

Reach out for help

It can be difficult for teenagers to learn to regulate their emotions on their own. If you are struggling to cope with stress or are feeling overwhelmed, it's important to talk to someone you trust. This person may not have an immediate solution to your problem, but communicating it can be calming on the mind and body. Building positive and supportive relationships can serve as a protective barrier against stress. Engaging with family or friends, participating in support groups, and seeking assistance from a professional counsellor are effective ways to reduce stress levels.

Practise meditation or mindfulness

Studies show that participating in meditation programmes can help minimise stress and improve your health. If you don't have time for a meditation programme, you can still practise mindfulness. Simple ways of doing this include focusing on the present moment and taking time to count your breaths.

Establish healthy habits

When you experience stress, getting enough sleep and eating well may be the last thing on your mind. However, getting a good night's rest and eating a balanced diet can help you cope with stressful situations. Because the teenage brain is growing and changing at a fast rate, it needs time to rest. Teenagers need between eight and ten hours of sleep a night for healthy brain function. Lack of sleep can affect emotional regulation and the ability to cope with stress.

Try to build some exercise into your daily routine. Exercise provides many physical and emotional benefits, including reducing stress and helping people to manage it better. Any movement, such as walking, cycling, yoga, weight training or team sports, can be a helpful stress-reliever and coping mechanism.

Spend time in nature

Research has found that spending time outdoors can boost your mood and help reduce stress. Taking a walk, going for a long cycle, or simply sitting outdoors to spend time in nature can help you relax and unwind.

ACTIVITY 19.2 – READ

In groups, read these three case studies and answer the questions that follow.

Case study 1

Dayna has been smoking for almost two years. However, she has recently been thinking about giving it up. The problem is, she has no idea where to start. She finds smoking really helpful for managing her anxiety, and she feels much more relaxed when she smokes.

1. Why does Dayna continue to smoke?
2. Do you think that smoking will help Dayna in the long run, physically and emotionally?
3. Suggest some positive coping strategies that Dayna could consider.

Case study 2

Theo has been out partying a lot lately. He has always drunk alcohol, but nowadays he has been feeling jittery and his anxiety seems to be getting worse. However, he loves going out and drinking, and doesn't want to stop.

1. Why is Theo becoming more anxious?
2. How do you think that Theo's dependency on alcohol will affect him in the long run?
3. Suggest some positive coping strategies that Theo could consider.

Case study 3

Viktoria used to smoke cannabis occasionally with her friends. However, she has lately started doing it alone too. It began as a way to relieve some stress, but now she feels like she needs to smoke to help her get through the day. She wants to seek help, but is too shy to speak about it in front of others.

1. Why does Viktoria continue to smoke cannabis?
2. Do you think that smoking cannabis will help Viktoria in the long run, physically and emotionally?
3. Suggest some positive coping strategies that Viktoria could consider.

ACTIVITY 19.3 – THINK

A. As a class, identify stressors in your lives and the positive coping strategies that can be used to deal with them. Consider the five ways to wellbeing while doing this activity:

BE ACTIVE   **TAKE NOTICE**   **KEEP LEARNING**   **GIVE**   **CONNECT**

Stressors	Positive coping strategies

B. Reflection questions:
1. Did you discover any new coping strategies today?
2. How do you feel about your ability to manage stress now?
3. What will you do differently to address stressors in your life?
4. What barriers exist that prevent us from using coping strategies? How do we overcome them?

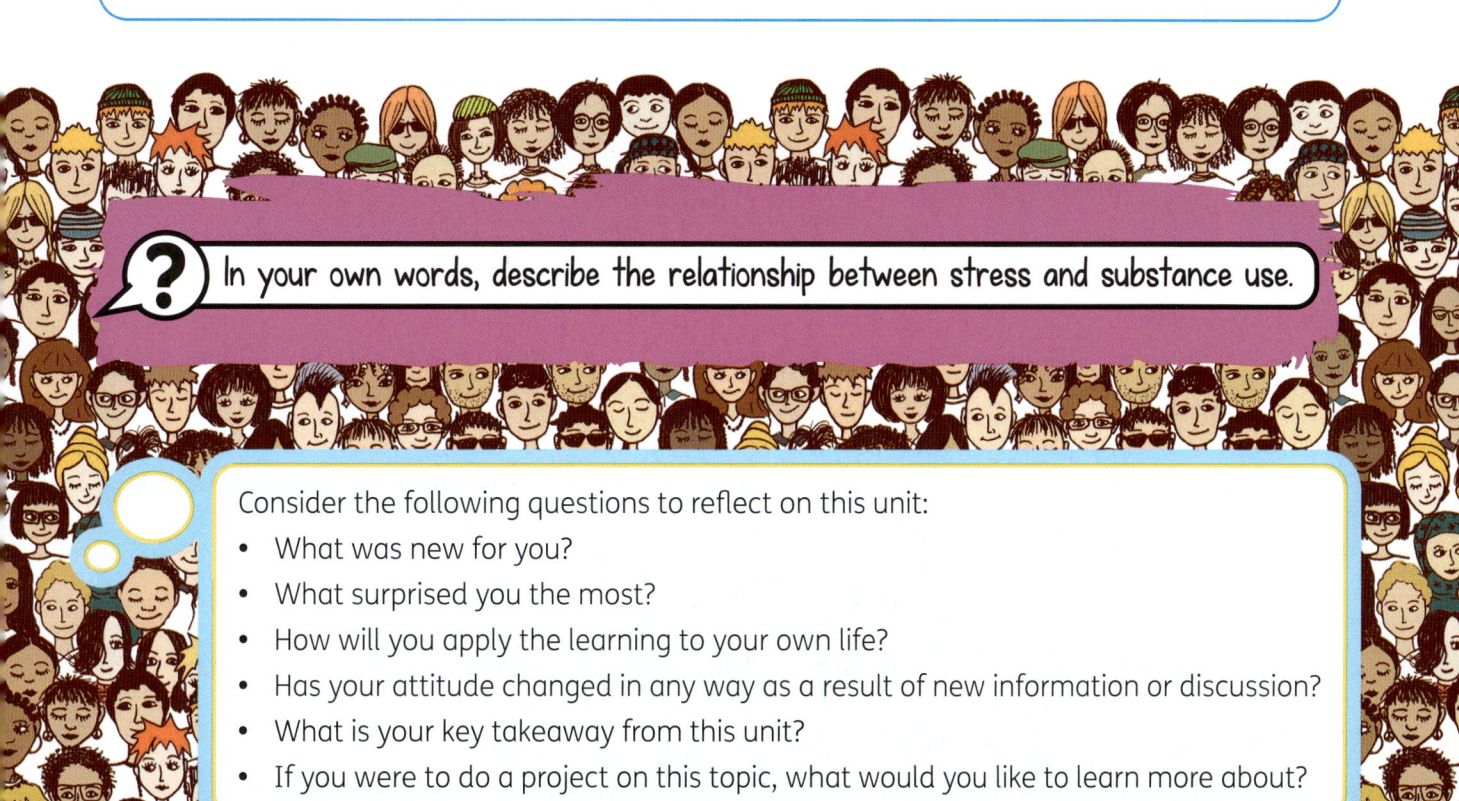

? In your own words, describe the relationship between stress and substance use.

Consider the following questions to reflect on this unit:
- What was new for you?
- What surprised you the most?
- How will you apply the learning to your own life?
- Has your attitude changed in any way as a result of new information or discussion?
- What is your key takeaway from this unit?
- If you were to do a project on this topic, what would you like to learn more about?

UNIT OF LEARNING 4

Intimate Relationships

The chapters in this Unit of Learning are:

- Chapter 20 – The Role of Intimacy and Pleasure in Relationships
- Chapter 21 – Consent in Intimate Relationships
- Chapter 22 – Pressures to Become Sexually Intimate
- Chapter 23 – Popular Culture and Sexual Expression
- Chapter 24 – What Is Pornography and Why Is It a Concern?
- Chapter 25 – The Impact of Pornography
- Chapter 26 – Ending Relationships

Note for teachers: This Unit of Learning engages with the following Learning Outcomes:

- **1.7** communicate in a respectful and effective manner and listen openly and sensitively to the views/feelings of others
- **1.9** demonstrate self-management skills, including setting personal goals, delaying gratification, and self-regulation of thoughts, emotions and impulses
- **3.1** reflect on the values, behaviours and skills that help to make, sustain and end relationships respectfully with friends, family and romantic/intimate relationships
- **3.2** examine benefits and difficulties experienced by young people in a range of relationships – friendships, family relationships, and romantic/intimate relationships
- **3.3** identify signs of healthy, unhealthy and abusive relationships
- **3.4** appreciate the importance of setting healthy boundaries in relationships and consider how to show respect for the boundaries of others
- **3.7** explore the pressures to become sexually intimate and discuss ways to show respect for people's choices
- **3.8** appreciate the importance of seeking, giving and receiving consent in sexual relationships, from the perspective of building caring relationships and from a legal perspective
- **3.10** discuss the influence of popular culture and the online world, in particular, the influence of pornography, on young people's understanding, expectations and social norms in relation to sexual expression
- **3.11** demonstrate how to access and appraise appropriate and trustworthy advice, support and services related to relationships and sexual health

Related Learning Outcomes: 1.7, 3.4, 3.7, 3.8.

CHAPTER 20

The Role of Intimacy and Pleasure in Relationships

In this chapter we will:
- discover the meaning of intimacy, both physical and emotional
- consider the various myths surrounding intimacy
- discuss the impact of positive and negative intimacy on relationships
- explore the term 'sexual pleasure'
- explore the steps involved in building intimacy.

KEY TERMS
Intimacy
Emotional intimacy
Positive intimacy
Negative intimacy
Sexual pleasure
Masturbation
Orgasm

? What words come to mind when you think of intimacy?

What is intimacy?

Intimacy is a broad term that describes physical and emotional closeness in different types of relationships, including romantic partnerships, friendships and family relationships. It's an important aspect of building healthy connections, and allows people to experience a sense of belonging with others. It can involve:

- sharing personal thoughts, feelings and experiences with someone you trust and care about
- being vulnerable and open with someone
- feeling understood and accepted
- **emotional intimacy**, which is a close emotional bond that includes emotional and intellectual connection. It features a deep sense of trust, vulnerability and closeness
- physical intimacy (e.g. hugging, holding hands, cuddling)
- sexual intimacy.

While sexual intimacy is a common feature of romantic relationships, intimacy can exist between partners without them engaging in sexual activity. For example, some people might want to wait until they're married or in a serious relationship before getting sexually intimate, and that's okay.

Building closeness and trust in a relationship takes time. It's important to get to know a person to fully understand what they are comfortable with.

ACTIVITY 20.1 – THINK

Read the following statements and indicate whether you believe each one is true or false. This activity can also be completed on the *You've Got This!* app.

	Statement	True	False
1	Intimacy is only about sexual activity.		✓
2	Intimacy is only for romantic relationships.		✓
3	Intimacy fades over time in long-term relationships.		✓
4	Intimacy means staying true to your values and only doing things you are comfortable with.	✓	
5	Intimacy is spontaneous and effortless.		✓
6	Intimacy can only be experienced in person.		✓
7	Intimacy is a one-size-fits-all concept.		✓
8	Building and nurturing intimacy requires open communication, trust, vulnerability and mutual respect.	✓	

Positive and negative intimacy

Positive intimacy involves building trust and closeness through mutual respect and understanding. When there is positive intimacy in your relationship, you feel safe to share your thoughts and feelings, knowing your boundaries are respected.

Negative intimacy occurs when boundaries are crossed or ignored. When there is negative intimacy in your relationship, you may feel uncomfortable, disrespected or betrayed.

ACTIVITY 20.2 – READ

In pairs, read these four case studies and answer the questions that follow.

Case study 1

Naoise and Quinn are in a romantic relationship. Quinn feels ready to take their relationship to the next level physically, but Naoise has expressed that they're not ready yet. Quinn respects this and decides to wait until Naoise feels comfortable.

1. How has Quinn demonstrated respect for Naoise's boundaries?
2. How does this respect contribute to positive intimacy in their relationship?

CHAPTER 20 – THE ROLE OF INTIMACY AND PLEASURE IN RELATIONSHIPS

Case study 2

Aaron and Kylie are dating. Aaron often makes comments about Kylie's appearance that make her feel uncomfortable and objectified (treated like an object or thing instead of a person). In particular, he regularly comments about her large breasts. When Kylie expresses her feelings, Aaron dismisses them. He says that she is overreacting and should take his comments as compliments.

1. How is Aaron's dismissal of Kylie's feelings affecting their intimacy?
2. How could Aaron respond differently to promote positive emotional and sexual intimacy in their relationship?

Case study 3

Daire and Clodagh have been dating for a while. They openly communicate about their comfort levels regarding physical intimacy, and regularly check in with each other to ensure they are both comfortable with the pace of their relationship.

1. What makes Daire and Clodagh's relationship an example of positive intimacy?
2. How does their approach to communication contribute to a healthy intimate relationship?

Case study 4

Ciaran and Marcia are in a romantic relationship. Marcia frequently shares her insecurities and anxieties with Ciaran, who listens and supports her without judgement. However, Ciaran never shares his feelings with Marcia, stating that he wants to stay strong for her.

1. How could the lack of emotional openness from Ciaran impact their intimacy in the long run?
2. What could Ciaran do to find balance in their emotional intimacy?

Sexual pleasure

Sexual pleasure is the physical and mental satisfaction and enjoyment that people experience from sexual activity. People of all different sexual identities can enjoy sexual pleasure.

There are many ways to experience sexual pleasure, both alone and with others:

Alone

Masturbation, also known as self-pleasure, is the stimulation of genital organs for sexual pleasure. Masturbation can lead to an **orgasm**, which is the physical and emotional sensation experienced at the peak of sexual excitement. Orgasm can also be achieved through other types of sexual activity.

Masturbation can be a pleasurable experience that:
- helps a person explore what they like sexually
- allows a person to connect with their body and develop good sexual health and attitudes
- brings relaxation, happiness and enjoyment to a person's life.

People can masturbate in many different ways. Some people choose not to masturbate or don't enjoy it, and this is okay. Each person's comfort with and experience of their own body is unique.

With others

Sexual pleasure can be experienced through sexual activities such as:
- kissing
- oral sex
- anal sex
- vaginal sex
- sex using hands and fingers
- masturbating together.

Some people choose not to experience sexual pleasure with others or don't enjoy it, and this is okay. Everyone has different comfort levels for engaging in sexual activities.

Sexual pleasure can also be experienced without any physical touching at all, through reading or watching something that causes arousal.

ACTIVITY 20.3 – DISCUSS

A. In groups, you will be given a set of intimacy cards that contain examples of different types of emotional and physical intimacy. Arrange the cards in the order of the steps involved in building intimacy, starting from the initial stages and progressing to the most intimate ones. You can place multiple cards at the same stage, and you don't have to use all the cards. Blank cards will also be available for you to write down any other examples you think of. Aim to reach a consensus as a group, and be prepared to justify your group's reasoning and decisions.

B. Reflection questions:
1. How did the process of ordering the intimacy cards challenge your understanding of building intimacy? Did physical or emotional cards take priority?
2. Were there any specific cards or stages that sparked interesting discussions within your group?
3. Reflecting on the cards you chose to include or set aside, what factors influenced your decisions? Did you consider personal experiences, societal expectations or other influences?
4. Did you encounter any difficulties or disagreements while trying to reach a consensus within your group? How did you navigate these challenges and what did you learn from the experience?
5. How does this activity deepen your understanding of the complexities of intimacy?
6. How can the insights gained from this activity be applied to your own life and relationships?

How has your understanding of intimacy, pleasure and the importance of boundaries in relationships changed after this chapter?

CHAPTER 21

Consent in Intimate Relationships

In this chapter we will:
- recap key terms on consent and sexual activity
- recognise the importance of asking for consent
- discuss the challenges of asking for consent and find ways to overcome them
- explore enthusiastic consent and its significance in sexual consent.

KEY TERMS
Verbal consent
Non-verbal consent
Enthusiastic consent
Implicit consent
Withdrawn consent
Non-consent

Related Learning Outcomes: 1.7, 3.4, 3.8.

? What does consent mean? What is the legal age of consent in Ireland?

ACTIVITY 21.1 – THINK

Think about what you have already learned about consent and sexual activity and fill in the blanks below.

| penis | fondling | vagina | pleasure | agreement | stimulation | alone |
| physical | anal | penetration | voluntary | anus | permission | intercourse |

1. Consent is when you agree to do something, or you give _____ for something to happen.
2. Sexual activity is a range of activities that involve giving or receiving _____. These activities can be done _____ or with other people, and include touching, _____, kissing and sexual _____.
3. Sexual intercourse refers to the _____ act of two people engaging in various sexual activities, which can include _____, oral or vaginal sex.
4. Anal sex involves the insertion of a _____ into the _____.
5. Oral sex refers to the _____ of the genitals using the mouth and tongue.
6. Vaginal sex involves the _____ of a _____ by a penis.
7. Sexual consent is the _____, mutual _____ between people involved in a sexual activity.

111

The importance of asking for consent

When engaging in a sexual activity, understanding consent means knowing that both people have agreed to engage in the activity and respect each other's limits. Asking for consent takes it a step further. It involves:

- actively seeking permission before engaging in any sexual activity
- ensuring that everyone involved is comfortable and enthusiastic.

Remember, consent is an ongoing process. Asking for consent is essential because it:

- is required by law (see page 119 for a reminder on consent and the law)
- empowers people to communicate their desires, boundaries and preferences
- supports open conversation
- promotes trust in relationships
- demonstrates care, consideration and respect for your partner.

ACTIVITY 21.2 – WATCH

Watch this video about asking for consent and answer the questions that follow.

▶ www.educate*plus*.ie/go/asking-consent

1. Is understanding consent easier than asking for it? Why?
2. What are the potential challenges or barriers that people may face when asking for sexual consent?
3. How can we overcome these challenges or barriers and create a culture in which asking for consent is normalised and encouraged?

Challenges when asking for consent

Asking for consent from a partner might feel challenging for the following reasons:

Challenges

- Movies, TV shows, music and society often send mixed messages about consent, making it seem unnecessary or uncool to ask for it.
- There is a fear of rejection or being judged.
- There is confusion about what consent is and when it's required.
- Asking for consent might make the situation or people involved feel awkward.
- It can be difficult to find the right words or phrases, which can make someone feel unsure or uncomfortable when asking for consent.

Verbal and non-verbal sexual consent

Verbal and non-verbal forms of sexual consent are essential communication methods. They establish mutual agreement and boundaries in intimate situations:

Verbal consent involves explicit communication through spoken or written words, where people clearly express their willingness to engage in specific sexual activities. It ensures that there is active participation and understanding for everyone involved.

Examples of verbal consent:

- Asking questions such as, 'May I kiss you?' or 'Are you comfortable with this?'
- Responding with words or phrases such as, 'Yes,' 'I want to,' or 'I'm okay with that.'

Non-verbal consent involves the use of body language, gestures and other non-verbal cues to indicate comfort, enthusiasm and willingness for sexual activity. Being attentive and using active listening is needed to understand these cues.

Examples of non-verbal consent:

- Positive body language such as leaning in, making eye contact or reciprocating (mutually giving and taking) physical touch.
- Nodding, smiling or showing signs of excitement or enthusiasm.

ACTIVITY 21.3 – READ

In pairs, read these four scenarios and answer the questions that follow.

Scenario 1

Barbara and Faye have been watching romantic movies in which consent is not discussed. The actors launch into sexual acts without saying a word to each other. After watching these movies, Barbara and Faye believe that non-verbal cues or assumptions are enough to understand and give consent.

1. How do you think the portrayal of consent in movies can impact our understanding of real-life consent?
2. What are some potential risks or misunderstandings that can arise from relying on non-verbal cues alone?
3. How can we challenge and change the misleading portrayal of consent in the media?

Scenario 2

Keith genuinely wants to seek consent, but struggles to find the right words or phrases to begin the conversation. He fears sounding awkward or ruining the mood.

1. How can we overcome the fear of sounding awkward or ruining the mood when discussing consent?
2. What are some alternative ways to start a conversation about consent without feeling uncomfortable?

Scenario 3

Karl feels nervous about asking his partner for consent because he worries about being judged or rejected by them. He believes that seeking consent might negatively impact his relationship and make things uncomfortable.

1. Why is it essential to prioritise consent over possible discomfort or awkwardness in a relationship?
2. How can we overcome the fear of being turned down when asking for consent?

Scenario 4

Lily struggles with seeking consent because she assumes that her partner will automatically know what she wants. She also feels uncomfortable asking for consent and relies on her partner to pick up on her physical cues.

1. What are the risks and challenges associated with relying on assumptions instead of seeking consent?
2. What strategies could be used to ensure that both partners actively seek and give consent throughout a sexual encounter?

Enthusiastic consent

Enthusiastic consent involves giving and receiving clear and excited confirmation to engage in a sexual activity. It goes beyond the absence of a 'No' – each person should actively seek a positive 'Yes' from their partner. Enthusiastic consent doesn't always have to be expressed verbally. Body language cues such as smiling, nodding and maintaining eye contact can be indicators of enthusiastic consent. However, verbal communication is still important when engaging in any sexual activity. Remember, consent can change. Keeping the conversation open is key, and each person should check in with their partner regularly.

Enthusiastic consent ensures that everyone's boundaries and choices are respected, and creates a safe and enjoyable experience.

ACTIVITY 21.4 – WATCH

A. Watch this video about enthusiastic consent to get a clearer understanding of its meaning:

▶ www.educate*plus*.ie/go/enthusiastic-consent

B. Share one new thing that you learned about enthusiastic consent from the video.

Other types of consent

Here are other types of consent that people may encounter in sexual situations:

Implicit consent: A person initiates a sexual activity assuming that consent is implied, based on their previous interactions.

Withdrawn consent: A person initially gives consent to engage in a sexual activity, but then changes their mind.

Non-consent: A person does not give any form of consent, is incapable of doing so, or is coerced (pressured) into it, and the other person proceeds with sexual activity against their will.

ACTIVITY 21.5 – THINK

A. In pairs, match the types of consent to the scenarios below.

1	Enthusiastic consent	A	Amelia initially agrees to engage in sexual activity with Mark, but later changes her mind and withdraws her consent. Mark respects her decision and immediately stops, understanding that consent can be taken back at any time.
2	Implicit consent	B	Isla and Kate are both enthusiastic about moving their relationship to another level together. They openly communicate what they are comfortable with, and express their excitement for the experience.
3	Withdrawn consent	C	Joshua expresses his discomfort and disinterest in any physical intimacy to his date. However, Patrick continues to make unwanted advances and ignores Joshua's clear non-verbal and verbal cues.
4	Non-consent	D	Jasmine and Ryan have been in a committed relationship for a while. They have a level of comfort and understanding that allows them to read each other's cues and non-verbal communication, so when Ryan leans in for a kiss to say goodbye, Jasmine responds by kissing him back.

1 = ___   2 = ___   3 = ___   4 = ___

B. Reflection questions:
1. What are the benefits and drawbacks of relying on assumptions within a relationship?
2. Does being in a long-term relationship mean that a person automatically consents to all forms of sexual activity?
3. How can explicit verbal communication contribute to a healthier dynamic in a relationship?
4. What strategies can be used to ensure there is clear and ongoing consent, even in long-term relationships?
5. Are there instances where non-verbal cues may not accurately reflect someone's consent?
6. How can we avoid making assumptions in relationships and prioritise open communication around consent?

? What steps can you take to ensure that there is clear communication and mutual understanding of consent in your current or future relationships?

Related Learning Outcomes: 1.7, 3.7, 3.8, 3.10.

CHAPTER 22

Pressures to Become Sexually Intimate

In this chapter we will:
- discuss the pressures to become sexually intimate
- explore the influence of music on teenagers' perceptions of sexual intimacy
- reflect on the term 'emotional readiness' and what it means to be emotionally ready for sexual intimacy
- consider ways to show respect for other people's choices.

KEY TERMS
Sexual intimacy
Sexual aggression
Dominance
Emotional readiness

? Think of a time when you felt pressured into doing something. How did it make you feel?

Sexual intimacy and pressures

Sexual intimacy refers to any physical or emotional act that is shared between individuals and involves a sexual nature. These acts can range from holding hands to engaging in sexual activity (e.g. kissing or having sexual intercourse). Sexual intimacy involves trust, emotional closeness and honest communication with a partner. It's a personal choice, and it should only happen when both people consent to it and feel safe and comfortable.

There are many internal and external factors that can influence and pressure people into becoming sexually intimate and active:

Internal factors
- Hormonal urges and sexual desires
- Emotional attachment or feelings of love towards a partner
- Desire for acceptance from a partner
- Fear of rejection or losing a relationship
- Curiosity about sexual experiences
- Desire to fit in
- Desire to explore sexuality
- Low self-esteem, or desire to find self-worth through sexual experiences
- FOMO (fear of missing out) and the fear of social exclusion
- Belief that engaging in sexual activity is a sign of maturity

External factors
- Influence from the media portraying idealised or exaggerated sexual relationships, and casual or frequent sexual encounters
- Pressure from romantic partners
- Influence from peers discussing their own sexual experiences or boasting about their number of sexual partners
- Pressure from society to conform to gender roles and expectations
- Pressure from advertising and marketing strategies that associate sexual activity with attractiveness and desirability
- Stigma or judgement from others for being 'sexually inexperienced'

ACTIVITY 22.1 – DISCUSS

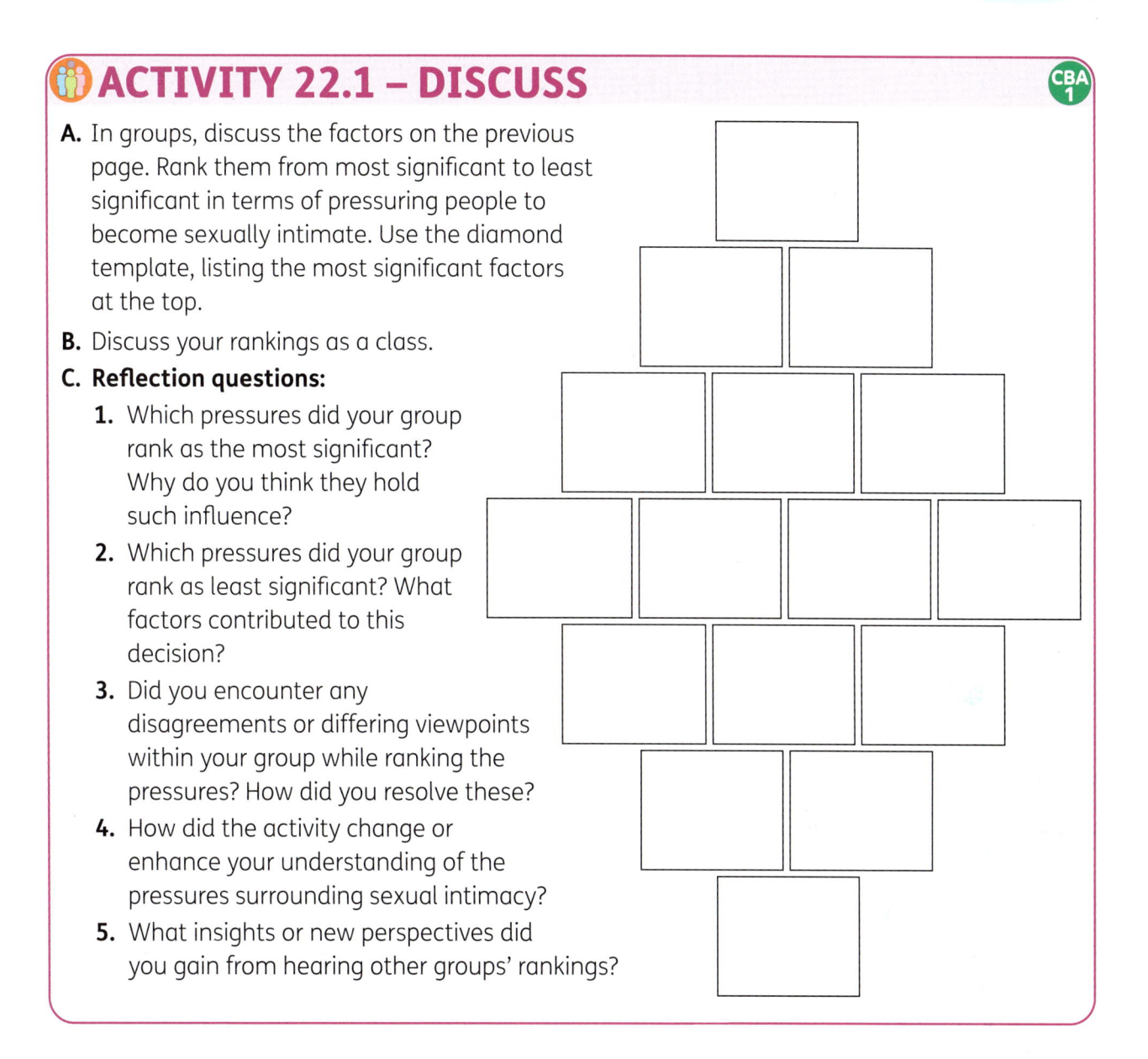

A. In groups, discuss the factors on the previous page. Rank them from most significant to least significant in terms of pressuring people to become sexually intimate. Use the diamond template, listing the most significant factors at the top.

B. Discuss your rankings as a class.

C. Reflection questions:
1. Which pressures did your group rank as the most significant? Why do you think they hold such influence?
2. Which pressures did your group rank as least significant? What factors contributed to this decision?
3. Did you encounter any disagreements or differing viewpoints within your group while ranking the pressures? How did you resolve these?
4. How did the activity change or enhance your understanding of the pressures surrounding sexual intimacy?
5. What insights or new perspectives did you gain from hearing other groups' rankings?

Influence of music on relationships

Music plays a large role in our everyday lives, and it can easily influence the way we think, behave and see the world. A lot of the music we listen to contains explicit sexual content. This content can affect how young people understand sexual intimacy by:

- shaping their attitudes, beliefs and decisions about sex and relationships
- putting pressure on them to engage in sexual activities.

Many popular songs today feature lyrics and music videos that make reference to sexual aggression and dominance.

Sexual aggression refers to behaviours that involve unwanted sexual advances or harassment. These include any actions or comments that make someone feel uncomfortable, violated or pressured into engaging in sexual activities.

Dominance refers to the power or control that one person may try to have over another.

It's very important to analyse the messages you receive from music. When you are aware of these messages and their influence, you have the power to make informed choices. Remember that what you see or hear in the media doesn't necessarily reflect real life.

ACTIVITY 22.2 – THINK

A. In pairs, choose one of the songs below and follow the corresponding link to read the lyrics. Then answer the questions that follow.

Song	Link
'Yes' by Beyoncé	www.educateplus.ie/go/beyonce-lyrics
'Unhealthy' by Anne-Marie	www.educateplus.ie/go/anne-marie-lyrics
'What Do You Mean?' by Justin Bieber	www.educateplus.ie/go/justin-bieber-lyrics
'Levitating' by Dua Lipa	www.educateplus.ie/go/dua-lipa-lyrics
'Animals' by Maroon 5	www.educateplus.ie/go/maroon-5-lyrics
'Your Power' by Billie Eilish	www.educateplus.ie/go/billie-eilish-lyrics

1. How do the lyrics of your chosen song influence people's perception of relationships? Can you identify specific lines or themes to support your answer?
2. What impact do you think songs like these can have on shaping attitudes and behaviours towards consent?

B. Take a moment to reflect on the type of music you listen to and the music videos you watch.
1. What subtle messages do you notice about sexual intimacy and expectations in relationships?
2. How do these messages influence your understanding of what sexual intimacy looks like?

C. Make a list of songs that show examples of behaviours that reflect healthy relationships.

Emotional readiness

Emotional readiness means being mentally and emotionally prepared to engage in an activity. It involves understanding your own feelings, boundaries and comfort levels. Emotional readiness plays a large role in sexual intimacy, and includes:

- communicating openly with your partner
- trusting your partner and feeling safe with them
- making sure you both want the same things
- listening to your partner
- considering the potential consequences
- thinking about your long-term goals.

Being emotionally ready allows you to make choices that prioritise your wellbeing and values.

People will experience emotional readiness at different stages of their lives. Here is an emotional readiness checklist to consider before engaging in sexual intimacy:

Emotional readiness checklist

- ☐ I understand my emotions, boundaries and comfort levels regarding sexual intimacy.
- ☐ I have good communication skills to express my feelings, desires and concerns with my partner openly and honestly.
- ☐ I have built a strong level of trust and mutual respect with my partner, and I feel safe and supported.
- ☐ I reflect on the potential consequences of sexual intimacy and think about whether I am prepared to handle them.
- ☐ I prioritise enthusiastic and ongoing consent from both me and my partner.
- ☐ I have a support network of trusted friends, family members or professionals who can provide guidance and assistance if needed.

CHAPTER 22 – PRESSURES TO BECOME SEXUALLY INTIMATE

ACTIVITY 22.3 – READ

Read these two case studies and answer the questions that follow.
A reminder on consent and the law is also provided.

Case study 1

Calum regularly watches music videos and TV shows that portray sexual intimacy as a spontaneous act that doesn't require any verbal consent. Recently, Calum was hanging out at a house party with Elisa, a girl from his year. Elisa and Calum started to chat and flirt. After a while, Calum felt a surge of arousal and pulled Elisa close to him, kissing her passionately. Elisa was taken by surprise but started to kiss him back. Calum then moved his hands over Elisa's breasts and fondled them, while Elisa continued to kiss him.

At a point, Calum suggested that they find a quieter spot behind the garden shed, to which Elisa agreed. Once behind the shed, Calum loosened Elisa's belt and put his hands down her trousers. He started whispering sexually explicit words in her ear as he did this, as this is what he had observed in music videos.

Case study 2

Sebastian frequently listens to songs that portray sexual aggression and dominance. He believes that the norm is for gay men to be attracted to forceful and dominant men. Over the past few months, Sebastian has developed feelings for his neighbour, Kayden. Kayden is aware of Sebastian's interest in him, but he isn't physically attracted to Sebastian. However, he feels pressured by his friends to have sex. They call him the 'virgin' of the group, and all seem to be sexually active. As a result of this pressure, Kayden decides to give Sebastian a chance.

One day, Kayden invites Sebastian over to his house to hang out. After some time, they start to kiss on the couch. Sebastian forcefully unbuttons Kayden's trousers, and Kayden is surprised by how forward he is. Sebastian then lowers Kayden's trousers and starts to give him oral sex.

Consent and the law

In Irish law, the Criminal Law (Sexual Offences) Act 2017 defines sexual consent. According to the Act, a person can give consent to a sexual act if they willingly agree to engage in it. However, there are situations where a person does not consent, including:

- when there is a threat of force
- when they are asleep or unconscious
- when they are unable to communicate due to alcohol or drug effects
- when they have a disability that affects communication
- when they are mistaken about the nature or purpose of the act
- when they are unlawfully detained (not allowed to leave)
- when someone else has given consent on their behalf.

The age of sexual consent in Ireland is 17 years. This applies to everyone, regardless of gender or sexual orientation.

1. How did media influences shape each teenager's perceptions of sexual intimacy and appropriate behaviour?
2. What are the potential consequences of their actions, in terms of consent? Are there legal consequences? (Refer to the 2017 Act above.)
3. What can we learn from these case studies about the potential impact of the media on our attitudes, beliefs and behaviours?

ACTIVITY 22.4 – CREATE

Rewrite the case studies from Activity 22.3 to reflect enthusiastic, ongoing and mutual consent. In each case study, ensure that you include ways of showing respect for others' choices.

Here are some tips to consider before deciding to engage in sexual activity:
- Remember that the legal age of consent in Ireland is 17 years. Anyone under 17 cannot legally consent to sexual activity.
- Talk openly about desires, boundaries and expectations before engaging in any sexual activity.
- Consider your emotions, feelings and readiness for intimate experiences.
- Treat your partner with respect, and honour their boundaries and wishes.
- Prioritise sexual health by using protection to prevent STIs and unwanted pregnancies.
- Trust yourself and listen to your instincts. If something doesn't feel right, it's okay to say 'no'.
- Reach out to trusted adults or professionals if you have questions or concerns.

What is your most important takeaway from this chapter?

Related Learning Outcomes: 1.9, 3.2, 3.10, 3.11.

CHAPTER 23

Popular Culture and Sexual Expression

In this chapter we will:
- define popular culture and sexual expression
- research factual information or statistics that debunk myths about popular culture and sexual expression
- explore how popular culture shapes sexual expression
- discuss ways to challenge popular culture when it doesn't reflect a person's needs and values.

KEY TERMS
Popular culture
Sexual expression
Casual hookup

? What movies and TV shows do you enjoy watching?

What is popular culture?

Popular culture refers to the set of ideas, trends and entertainment that is widely embraced by society and influences the way people think and behave. Examples of popular culture include:

- music
- movies
- TV shows
- video games
- social media
- fashion
- magazines
- literature
- art
- poetry.

Popular culture plays a significant role in shaping our perceptions of sex. In this fast-paced media age, we are bombarded with messages and images that often set unrealistic standards and expectations of sex and relationships. These messages and images can also influence our understanding of **sexual expression**, which refers to:

- different sexual behaviours
- sexual desire (the wish to engage in sexual activities)
- arousal
- lust (feelings of sexual desire for someone).

We have the power to think for ourselves and question the influences of popular culture. By understanding how popular culture can shape our thoughts, beliefs and actions, we can make choices that truly matter to us in relationships.

ACTIVITY 23.1 – DISCUSS

A. Below are some myths about popular culture and sexual expression. In groups, research one of the myths and find factual information or statistics that debunk it (show that it's false). Use the tips on how to access trustworthy information to help you.

Myths	
1. All music lyrics reflect healthy relationships and consent.	2. Celebrities and influencers always have healthy and ideal relationships.
3. Sexualised clothing and appearance play an important role in attractiveness.	4. Romantic comedies always present healthy relationship dynamics.
5. The media glamorises the idea of having casual hookups without consequences. A **casual hookup** is a short, physical relationship between people who don't wish for an emotional connection or long-term commitment.	6. Sexual content in the media has no impact on teenagers' sexual attitudes and behaviours.
7. Popular culture encourages open communication and consent in sexual relationships.	

Tips for accessing trustworthy information:

- Use reliable sources, such as educational websites or respected organisations, that focus on topics like relationships and sexuality. These sources often provide accurate and age-appropriate information.
- Check for verified references at the bottom of online articles to ensure that the information is backed up by actual research.
- Look for surveys or polls conducted by well-known organisations that ask people about their beliefs and attitudes towards sexual expression. These surveys can highlight common misconceptions or myths in popular culture.
- Evaluate the expertise of the author or contributors providing the advice. Check if they have relevant qualifications or experience in the area.
- If something doesn't feel right or align with your own values or experiences, trust your instincts and look for other perspectives. It's a good idea to consult multiple sources to gain a broader understanding of the topic.

B. Present your findings to the class. After every group has presented, have a class discussion about how these myths can put pressure on teenagers and shape their behaviours.

How does popular culture shape sexual expression?

Here are some examples of how popular culture shapes sexual expression:

Idealised unhealthy relationship dynamics

Movies, TV shows and songs tend to glamorise possessiveness, jealousy and toxic behaviours as signs of passionate love. This can create the belief that these behaviours are normal or even something to seek in relationships, which can lead to unhealthy and harmful relationship expectations.

CHAPTER 23 – POPULAR CULTURE AND SEXUAL EXPRESSION

'Hookup culture'
Popular culture often represents casual sexual encounters as the norm, and places less emphasis on emotional connection and commitment. This can create pressure on people to engage in casual sex without considering their desires, boundaries or emotional readiness.

Gender stereotypes
Popular culture often places a strong focus on traditional gender stereotypes relating to sex and sexuality. For instance, men are often portrayed as sexually aggressive and dominant, while women are often treated like objects. These stereotypes can influence how people perceive their own roles and expectations in sexual relationships.

Influence on body image and sexual confidence
Popular culture's emphasis on physical appearance can impact body image and sexual confidence. It can make people feel insecure about their bodies, and lead them to conform to certain beauty standards in order to feel desirable or worthy of sexual attention.

Instant sexual gratification
Popular culture often promotes the idea of instant sexual gratification, where sex is portrayed as a quick and effortless source of pleasure. This creates unrealistic expectations of sexual experiences, and also ignores the importance of emotional connection and consent.

ACTIVITY 23.2 – DISCUSS

Elona loves writing poems and often spends her Saturday mornings lost in her poetry. During one of her writing sessions, she reflected on how popular culture shapes sexual expression and wrote the following poem.

In pairs, read Elona's poem and answer the questions that follow each stanza.

> In a world of silver screens, illusions hold their sway,
> Romanticising love, but leading hearts astray.
> Possessiveness means passion, control means true desire,
> But these acts of 'love' are toxic – not something to admire.

1. Have you ever noticed possessiveness and jealousy being portrayed as signs of love in movies or songs?
2. How do you think this affects our understanding of healthy relationships?

> In the grip of hookup culture, we dance on fragile strings,
> No commitment, no emotions – only temporary flings.
> Seeking thrills and something 'casual', we bounce from date to date,
> But can we rise above these norms, and redefine our fate?

3. How does popular culture's emphasis on hookup culture impact the way we approach our relationships, desires and boundaries?
4. How can we build meaningful and lasting connections with others?

We can challenge our perceptions and ignite a different flame,
Where emotional connection and consent are not a game.
Instant pleasure and rewards can throw a veil over our eyes,
Making love seem like a challenge, and a thing to compromise.

> 5. How does popular culture affect our understanding of intimacy and consent?
> 6. How can we prioritise emotional connection over instant gratification?

Gender stereotypes, the masks we wear, define our gender roles.
Men are 'leaders' in society, women are 'objects' to control.
Can we break these chains to build a world that's equal and fair?
Or will we judge a person based on who they are and what they wear?

> 7. How do gender stereotypes affect our understanding of sexuality and relationships?
> 8. How can we challenge and redefine these stereotypes?

In a world of false ideals, we see 'beauty' on our screens.
Flawless smiles and stunning bodies aim to hurt our self-esteem.
If we celebrate our bodies and embrace our true reflections,
We'll find value in uniqueness and accept our imperfections.

> 9. How does popular culture's emphasis on physical appearance influence our body image?
> 10. How can we create a positive sense of self despite this influence?

ACTIVITY 23.3 – READ

Read these diary entries and answer the questions that follow.

Diary entry 1: Jean's perspective

Dear Diary,

I feel torn between what I've learned from popular culture and my own values and emotions. Everywhere I look, casual hookups are shown as exciting and glamorous. It seems like everyone around me is talking about their casual encounters and the thrill of living in the moment. I find myself questioning if I should also be having these experiences.

Diary entry 2: Brody's perspective

Dear Diary,

It's been a confusing time lately. I'm trying to figure out this idea of hookup culture that seems to be everywhere. There's a focus on casual sexual activity without emotional commitment. The songs I listen to make it seem like hooking up is what everyone does, and anything more serious is old-fashioned.

1. How is popular culture affecting Jean and Brody?
2. How can Jean and Brody make choices that match what they feel inside?

> Has this chapter made you more aware of the influence of popular culture on your choices, values and wellbeing? How?

Related Learning Outcomes: 1.7, 1.9, 3.1, 3.2, 3.10.

CHAPTER 24

What Is Pornography and Why Is It a Concern?

In this chapter we will:
- define pornography
- learn about the impact of pornography on the teenage brain
- discuss how pornography can negatively affect romantic relationships.

KEY TERMS
Pornography
Uncensored consent

? What comes to mind when you hear the term 'pornography'?

ACTIVITY 24.1 – THINK

In your opinion, which of these descriptions best reflects the meaning of pornography? Take a class vote.

1	Pornography is content that explores and promotes healthy sexual relationships. It also educates individuals about sexual health and consent.	3	Pornography is media content that shows sexual acts or nudity for the purpose of adult entertainment and sexual gratification (pleasure).
2	Pornography is any form of media that showcases nudity (nakedness) or sexual content, regardless of its intent or audience.	4	Pornography is a type of art that explores and celebrates human sexuality in a tasteful manner.

What is pornography?

Pornography (or porn for short) is adult content that shows sexual images or videos of naked bodies or sexual acts. It comes in various forms, including:
- printed materials such as magazines
- online content available on websites or social media platforms
- streaming videos.

The purpose of pornography is to arouse sexual feelings or excitement. It's created for adults and is not meant to be accessed or watched by children or teenagers.

125

Pornography does not accurately represent real-life experiences, and important features of healthy relationships (communication, trust and consent) are often not shown. Watching pornography may give people unrealistic expectations about body image, sexual activity and performance. It may also affect how they see and behave around others. The use of contraception is rarely, if ever, discussed in pornography.

ACTIVITY 24.2 – WATCH

Watch this video about why young people may watch pornography and answer the questions that follow.

▶ www.educateplus.ie/go/online-pornography

1. Why might some people think pornography is a good way to learn about sex?
2. Sadie says that 'everyone goes along with it' and watches pornography. Do you agree with this statement?
3. Sadie mentions that some boys at her school 'genuinely think porn is real'. Do you think that her statement applies to many young people in general?
4. How might mistaking pornography for real life affect someone's understanding of sexual activity?

Pornography and the teenage brain

During adolescence, the brain is still developing. This makes it more vulnerable to the influence of **uncensored content**, which is unedited material that includes information, words or images that might be considered controversial, explicit or sensitive. Exposure to uncensored content such as pornography can shape a teenager's attitudes and behaviours around sex and relationships.

Adolescence is also a time for learning emotional regulation and developing healthy expectations for intimacy. Regularly viewing pornography may affect a teenager's emotional regulation skills and alter their understanding of healthy relationships and consent. Research suggests that regularly viewing pornography during adolescence may increase the risk of developing issues with sexual behaviours or sexual addiction later in life.

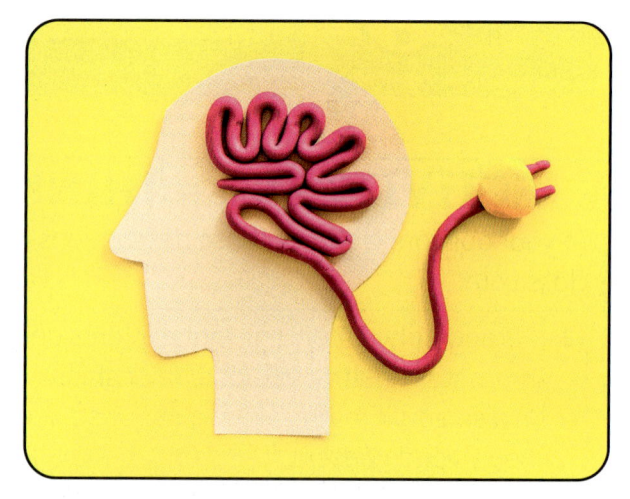

ACTIVITY 24.3 – WATCH

Watch this video about pornography and reality. Write down one thing that surprised you from the video.

▶ www.educateplus.ie/go/pornography-and-reality

CHAPTER 24 – WHAT IS PORNOGRAPHY AND WHY IS IT A CONCERN?

ACTIVITY 24.4 – READ

A. In pairs, read this timeline that outlines Julian's experience with pornography and answer the questions that follow.

Age 13	Julian was hanging out with his friends after school one day. One of his friends handed him his phone and said, 'Check this out.' Julian wasn't expecting to be shown pornography, and he was quite shocked and disturbed by what he saw.
Age 14	Julian started to hear more of his friends talking about pornography. They were using sexual terms and slang that he didn't understand. When his friend sent him a video of pornography, he started watching it so that he could have the same knowledge as his friends. He didn't want them to realise that he didn't know what they were talking about.
Age 15	By the age of 15, Julian was watching pornography quite frequently. He no longer only watched what his friends sent him – he started to look it up online himself. He even started to share some clips with his friends.
Age 16	By the age of 16, Julian was watching pornography daily. The pornography that he was watching was also changing, as he wasn't getting the same level of arousal as he used to. The content was now becoming much more aggressive. Up until this point, Julian had been too shy to talk to girls, and he had never had a girlfriend. However, Nichola, a girl in his year, started to chat with him at lunch time. He was delighted, despite feeling nervous. After some time, they started to hang out at the weekends. One evening, Julian felt aroused when he put his arm around Nichola. He turned to her and started to forcefully kiss her. Nichola was shocked and pushed him back. She then told him to leave. Julian left, feeling confused and upset by her reaction. After that, Nichola refused to talk to Julian at school. His friends made jokes about the situation, saying that Julian 'couldn't keep a woman for more than five seconds'.

1. Julian felt shocked and disturbed when he first saw pornography. Who could he have talked to about these feelings?
2. What are some negative effects of sharing pornography with friends?
3. How do you think Julian's exposure to pornography affected his feelings and thoughts about normal sexual behaviour?
4. How did Julian's taste in pornography change over time?
5. How did watching pornography affect Julian's relationship with Nichola?
6. What could Julian have done to learn about sex instead of watching pornography?

B. In pairs, discuss and list the potential outcomes or consequences for Julian in each of these scenarios:

Scenario 1: Julian continues to regularly watch aggressive pornography.	**Scenario 2:** Julian recognises the negative influences of pornography on his perception of sex.

ACTIVITY 24.5 – THINK

Your teacher will designate four corners of the room as 'Agree', 'Disagree', 'Don't know' and 'Neutral'. They will then read out a number of statements. When asked, move to the corner of the room that reflects your opinion on the statement.

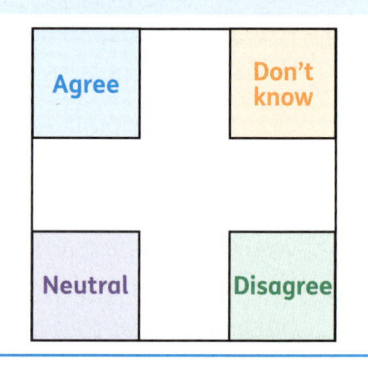

? Identify one important thing that you have learned from this chapter.

Related Learning Outcomes: 1.9, 3.1, 3.2, 3.10.

CHAPTER 25

The Impact of Pornography

In this chapter we will:
- explore why young people may view pornography
- examine different attitudes, beliefs and opinions about pornography
- understand the effects of viewing pornography
- explore how pornography can affect sexual preferences in relationships
- offer advice to teenagers who have been exposed to pornography.

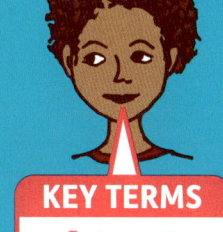

KEY TERMS
Internet pornography

> Based on what you have learned so far, what impacts do you think pornography can have on people?

Teenage curiosity and pornography

It's natural to be curious about sex. From puberty onwards, most people's brains are wired to be interested in it, even if they're not emotionally ready to engage in sexual activity. Curiosity often leads young people to search the internet for more information, which can result in them discovering pornography. Under Irish law, individuals under the age of 18 are classified as children. Pornography is intended for adults aged 18 and over.

Since around 2008, **internet pornography** has become widely and easily accessible. Advancements in technology have made pornography readily available in large quantities and on different platforms and websites. The increase in online pornographic content has made it easier for young people to be exposed to explicit images and videos, both willingly and unwillingly. Much of the content can be intense, which can overwhelm young, developing minds and create cravings to seek out more.

ACTIVITY 25.1 – ROLE PLAY

A. In this activity, your class will role play a courtroom scene in which pornography is put on trial. The classroom should be arranged to mirror a courtroom layout:

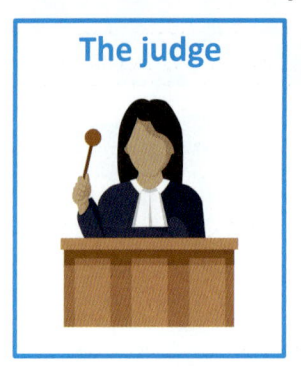

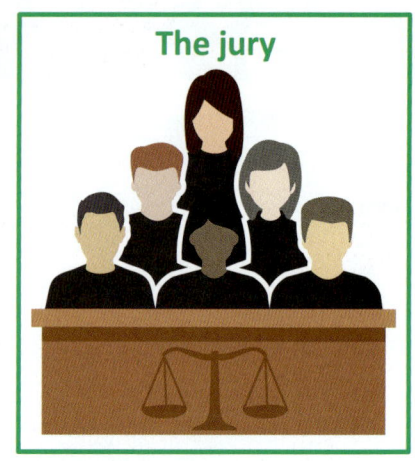

Four people giving evidence
- Dr Peterson, a neuroscientist
- Dr Davis, a psychologist
- Lisa, an ethical porn producer
- Dr Johnson, a GP

The judge

The jury

The lawyers
- Lawyer 1
- Lawyer 2
- Lawyer 3
- Lawyer 4

Your teacher will assign students to the following roles and share role play scripts with them:
- The judge, who will oversee the trial.
- The four lawyers, who will each question one of the people giving evidence.
- The four people giving evidence, who will answer the questions they are asked.
- The jury, who will listen to each case presented. The jury will be made up of the remaining students.

B. Reflection questions:
1. How has engaging in this activity deepened your understanding of the issues surrounding pornography?
2. Was there any information shared that challenged your beliefs about pornography?
3. After listening to the arguments presented in the courtroom trial, what do you think are the dangers of watching pornography?

ACTIVITY 25.2 – WATCH

Watch this video about the impact of pornography and answer the questions that follow.

▶ www.educate*plus*.ie/go/porn-problems

1. At what age did Gabe start watching pornography?
2. At what age did Gabe realise that pornography was having a negative effect on him?
3. Gabe calls pornography a 'normal part of teen culture'. Do you agree? Why?
4. If Gabe knew at the age of 12 that pornography would impact his relationships later in life, do you think he would have made different decisions?

CHAPTER 25 – THE IMPACT OF PORNOGRAPHY

ACTIVITY 25.3 – READ

A. Read this conversation between two teenagers, **Cameron** and **Robin**, in which they discuss consent in their relationship.

Cameron: Hey Robin, can we chat about something?

Robin: Sure, what's up?

Cameron: I've been thinking about the whole consent thing since we covered it in class. You and I don't talk about consent, and we've been together for a while.

Robin: Okay, what do you want to talk about?

Cameron: Well, we're getting more serious, so we should probably talk about sex and what we are and aren't comfortable with. What do you think?

Robin: It's not something I'm used to talking about, but yeah, it makes sense. I really like you and I want this relationship to work, so it's good to discuss this.

Cameron: Yeah, I feel the same. So, what should we expect from each other when we have sex? Like, there are lots of graphic things shared online that don't make sex look enjoyable.

Robin: Do you mean porn?

Cameron: Yeah. It can be really disturbing to watch. And it's so unrealistic. I mean, the men usually have six packs and huge muscles!

Robin: And the women have these 'perfect' model bodies that are completely clean shaven!

Cameron: I also don't like how men come across as really dominant and forceful, and women are expected to accept it. This can't be what people really enjoy, can it?

Robin: Surely not. I remember learning in class that porn doesn't reflect real life and it never shows people consenting to sex or using contraception.

Cameron: So how can we make sure that we're both comfortable when we're being intimate? For example, I really don't want to be forceful when we're kissing. I'd be afraid I'd hurt you!

Robin: You're right – I wouldn't like that! We can be intimate in a gentle way.

Cameron: I agree. I think intimacy is about connection, trust and communication. We should focus on what makes us feel happy, rather than trying to copy something we see in porn.

➡ *Continued on next page.*

Robin: Definitely. And consent is important too. For me, consent means that we're both totally cool with what's happening and we're both into it.

Cameron: Yeah, consent should be something we're both genuinely excited about.

Robin: And it's not just a one-time thing, you know? We should be able to say 'stop' or 'no' at any point.

Cameron: Totally. It's okay to change our minds if we're not feeling it. And I hope you'd let me know if I ever do something that makes you uncomfortable.

Robin: I would. I always feel safe around you. But I was wondering, how would you feel about having some kind of signal or check-in? Like using a safe word or just asking, 'Are you okay with this?'

Cameron: I like that idea. It's a good way to make sure we're both comfortable.

Robin: And like we learned in class, consent doesn't just have to be about words. We can show it through body language. If one of us looks unsure or uneasy, the other should back off if needed.

Cameron: I completely agree. I feel like we know each other's body language really well, but it's still important to be aware and check in.

Robin: Exactly. Like, if I'm smiling and cuddling up to you, that's a sign I'm in the mood to be affectionate. But if I'm tired or distracted, I'll be a bit more distant and want my own space.

Cameron: That's really good to know. We should both respect each other's boundaries and limits. And we should never pressure each other into doing something we're not into, despite porn showing us what's 'normal'.

Robin: You're right. I'm so glad we had this chat – thanks for bringing it up! I don't think I would have been brave enough to.

Cameron: It feels good to talk about this! I'm happy that we're on the same page about things.

Robin: Same here! So, to put our words into action – can I give you a kiss?

Cameron: Yes!

B. Reflection questions:

1. What key aspects of healthy communication about consent did you observe in Cameron and Robin's conversation?
2. Why do you think it's important for couples to have open discussions about consent and boundaries in their relationships?
3. How can clear communication and consent enhance intimacy and trust in a relationship, especially when discussing unrealistic expectations from pornography?

CHAPTER 25 – THE IMPACT OF PORNOGRAPHY

ACTIVITY 25.4 – READ

In groups, read the four scenarios and the nine pieces of advice below. Suggest which piece of advice you think will help the teenager in each scenario. Give a reason for each choice. If you think of a more appropriate or effective piece of advice than those listed, share it with the class.

Scenario	Piece of advice
Ethan, aged 16, uses pornography as a way to cope with stress and loneliness. While it offers temporary relief, Ethan has noticed that it negatively affects his mood and self-esteem.	① Seek guidance from a trusted adult to help you better understand your feelings around the uncensored content. ② Trust your instincts and choose friends who respect your boundaries and choices. ③ Explore healthier coping mechanisms for stress, such as taking up a hobby or talking to someone you trust about your emotions.
Grace, aged 15, accidentally stumbles upon uncensored sexual content while browsing the internet. She feels confused and uncomfortable about what she sees.	④ Be critical of online information and discuss any concerns with a trusted adult who can guide you towards reliable resources. ⑤ Understand that accidental exposure isn't your fault, and talk to a parent or guardian for support. ⑥ Prioritise your values and seek friendships with like-minded people who share your values.
Peadar, aged 15, is pressured by his friends to watch pornography and to join in their conversations about it. He feels uncertain about joining in.	⑦ Seek reliable resources for accurate information about relationships and sexuality, rather than relying on pornography. ⑧ Research how the brain reacts to pornography to get a better understanding of its effects on the teenage brain. ⑨ Speak to an adult about adjusting the settings on your devices to prevent accidental exposure to sexual content.
Rose, aged 16, becomes curious about pornography after hearing their friends talk about it. They wonder if watching it will provide insights into relationships.	

TIPS

Here are some tips to follow if you become exposed to pornography:
- Question the unrealistic portrayals of sex in pornography and recognise that it doesn't reflect real-life relationships.
- Educate yourself about sex and relationships from reliable sources that promote healthy values and consent.
- Know your comfort level and communicate openly with partners about what you are and aren't comfortable with.
- Value yourself and others, ensuring that all sexual encounters are consensual and respectful.
- Surround yourself with friends who encourage healthy attitudes towards sex and relationships.

? List your three most important takeaways from this chapters.

Related Learning Outcomes: 3.1, 3.3, 3.11.

CHAPTER 26

Ending Relationships

In this chapter we will:
- explore why relationships end
- recognise the warning signs of abuse in a relationship
- discuss coercive control
- discuss how to end relationships respectfully
- explore the emotional impacts of ending relationships.

KEY TERMS
Abusive relationship
Domestic abuse
Coercive control

? Why do relationships end?

Why relationships end

People end relationships for many reasons. For example:

- They may be unhappy in their relationship.
- They do not enjoy it anymore.
- They find their values shifting in different directions.
- There is a breakdown in communication or trust.
- They are separated by long distances.
- They decide that they're better off as friends.
- They simply want something different in life.

A lot of the time, relationships can end on good terms, but many people go through difficult break-ups, and this can be an upsetting and challenging time.

Ending a relationship is often necessary for people's emotional wellbeing. However, there may be instances when a relationship can be worked on, with good communication and commitment from both sides.

ACTIVITY 26.1 – DISCUSS

A. In pairs, read through the scenarios below and decide where along the relationship spectrum each relationship best belongs. Give reasons for each decision.

Relationship spectrum

Work through it Take a break It's complicated Break up completely

Scenario 1
Mila recently found out that her boyfriend, Darragh, lied about where he was at the weekend. He said he was visiting family, but Mila learned from a friend that he actually went to a party. Now, Mila questions whether she can trust Darragh, and Darragh feels like Mila is constantly checking up on him.

Scenario 2
Tommy and Carey have been together for a year. Initially, they shared many common interests, but lately, they've found their interests differ. Tommy is getting more involved in sports, while Carey has developed a passion for music and acting. They find themselves spending less time together and more time with friends who share their new interests.

Scenario 3
Bridget and Toby are in a relationship, but Toby's friends disapprove. They make fun of him for being in a relationship and pressure him to hang out with them more. Toby starts to feel torn between his friends and Bridget, leading to tension in the relationship.

Scenario 4
Saibh and Seamus have been dating for several months. They trust each other and have shared intimate moments together. Recently, Saibh showed an intimate photo of them to her best friend without Seamus' consent, and told her friend not to tell anyone. However, Seamus heard rumours about the picture and asked Saibh if she had shared it. Saibh confessed that she did, but that she never intended for it to become public. Seamus felt hurt and betrayed, and now doesn't know if he can be intimate with Saibh anymore.

B. What advice would you give to each partner in the scenarios? Make notes in your copy and discuss your answers in pairs.

Abusive relationships

Sometimes, relationships can become abusive. An **abusive relationship** is a harmful and dangerous relationship that features physical, verbal, emotional or sexual abuse. If your partner or former partner makes you feel scared or intimidated, or displays controlling behaviour, this is an abusive relationship.

In an abusive relationship, the abuser tries to dominate and manipulate their partner. This can cause:

- fear
- worry
- self-doubt
- low self-esteem
- anxiety
- isolation.

All forms of abuse are damaging, and no one deserves to be treated in this way. Sometimes, a relationship that starts off as healthy can evolve into an abusive relationship. Learning to recognise abuse in a relationship is the first step to getting help.

An abusive relationship can include **domestic abuse**, which is abuse that takes place in the home between intimate partners. It can include physical violence, emotional abuse, verbal abuse, sexual abuse, financial abuse and isolation.

Being in an abusive relationship can be harmful for people's emotional, physical and mental wellbeing. These types of relationships should be ended as soon as possible.

Warning signs of abuse

Below is a list of red flags (warning signs) that can indicate an abusive relationship. All of these signs are serious, and a person does not have to experience several or all of them to be in an abusive relationship.

You could be in an abusive relationship if your partner …

- 🚩 complains when you spend time with friends and family, and makes you feel guilty for not spending all your free time with them
- 🚩 calls you names, insults you or humiliates you
- 🚩 sends continuous texts and becomes angry if you don't respond immediately
- 🚩 tells you how you should dress and criticises your clothing choices
- 🚩 has a bad temper, causing you to fear disagreeing with them
- 🚩 is very jealous and frequently accuses you of cheating on them
- 🚩 demands access to your phone to read your messages, and presses you for your passwords
- 🚩 pressures you into engaging in sexual activities you are uncomfortable with
- 🚩 is physically violent towards you
- 🚩 controls everything in your life, such as where you go, who you see or how you spend your money.

CHAPTER 26 – ENDING RELATIONSHIPS

ACTIVITY 26.2 – READ

In groups, read these two case studies and answer the questions that follow.

Case study 1

Elaine has been seeing Eoin for several months. She has strong feelings for him, and feels fortunate that he wants to be with her. However, Eoin frequently gets angry with her when she interacts with other guys. It upsets her when he gets angry, and she finds herself apologising for her actions in the hope that he won't leave her. When he's not angry, he's very loving and caring towards her.

At a disco recently, a few different boys tried to flirt with Elaine. She felt guilty about this, even though she wasn't flirting back. She knew that it would make Eoin feel embarrassed and jealous, and she was worried that he would be angry if he heard. She regretted wearing her short skirt and calling attention to herself.

1. How does Elaine feel about her relationship with Eoin?
2. What are the signs of abuse in this relationship?
3. How is Eoin's behaviour affecting Elaine?
4. If you were Elaine's best friend, what advice would you give her?

Case study 2

Harry and Finlay have been in a relationship for two years. At the start, everything seemed perfect. However, Finlay's behaviour slowly began to change over time. He is now possessive and controlling, monitoring Harry's every move. He gets angry if Harry spends time with friends or family without him. He also insists on knowing Harry's whereabouts at all times. As a result of Finlay's behaviour, Harry has stopped seeing his friends and has become more distant with his family.

Finlay's controlling behaviour has extended to Harry's appearance. He criticises Harry's clothing choices and asks him not to wear certain things. This has made Harry lose confidence in himself.

Harry blames himself for Finlay's behaviour, thinking that he must have done something to provoke him. He has often thought about ending the relationship. However, whenever they argue, Finlay apologises for the way he's been acting and promises not to do it again. This gives Harry hope that things will get better.

1. How does Harry feel about his relationship with Finlay?
2. What are the signs of abuse in this relationship?
3. How is Finlay's behaviour affecting Harry?
4. Why do you think Harry remains in this relationship?
5. What advice would you give to someone in Harry's position?

Coercive control

Coercive control is a common feature in abusive relationships. It involves persuading or forcing someone to do something by using threats and intimidation. Coercive control aims to:

- make a person dependant on their partner
- isolate a person from others
- make a person afraid to leave the relationship or to speak out
- restrict a person's behaviour and freedom
- damage a person's self-esteem.

Coercive control can make a person feel constantly on edge, as they try to please their partner to avoid conflict or punishment. When the person being controlled tries to leave, their partner will likely threaten to hurt them, themselves or others.

Examples of coercive control include:

- isolating a person from friends and family
- excessively texting, calling or using social media to monitor a person's whereabouts and activities
- constantly criticising, belittling or shaming a person
- emotional manipulation – guilt-tripping or playing the victim to manipulate a person's feelings and behaviour
- making a person engage in sexual activity
- enforcing rules and activities that humiliate a person
- threatening to reveal or publish private information about a person, such as posting private photos or videos online.

ACTIVITY 26.3 – DISCUSS

A. The class will be divided into four groups. Each group will be assigned one of the scenarios on the next page. Read through your assigned scenario and make notes on the following:

1. Is there evidence of controlling behaviour? If so, highlight examples.
2. What actions could the person take to manage the situation?
3. What do you think the outcome of each scenario will be based on the questions asked at the end?

CHAPTER 26 – ENDING RELATIONSHIPS

B. Pass your notes to the group beside you. Each group should read through the notes that have been given to them and add any further insights or advice they have. Repeat this until each group has had a chance to make notes on each of the four scenarios.

Scenario 1

Dora and Christopher have been dating for a few months. Christopher becomes increasingly controlling and starts discouraging Dora from spending time with her friends. He insists on knowing her whereabouts all the time, and guilt-trips her when she wants to go out with her friends without him. Dora feels isolated and suffocated, torn between wanting to maintain her friendships and keeping Christopher happy.

Will Dora confront Christopher about his behaviour and set boundaries, or will she end the relationship to regain her freedom?

Scenario 2

Marley and Olive have been together for a year. Marley becomes possessive and insecure, constantly checking Olive's phone for messages and social media interactions. Olive's social life becomes a constant point of disagreement, leading to arguments and distrust. Olive feels suffocated by Marley's constant monitoring, but still cares for them deeply.

Will Marley recognise their controlling behaviour and seek to change it, or will Olive break up with them to find a healthier and more trusting relationship?

Scenario 3

Megan and Ryan have been dating for a while. Ryan starts demanding Megan's social media passwords and constantly monitors her online interactions. He gets upset over harmless likes and comments from other people. Megan feels like she's being smothered and starts hiding things from Ryan to avoid conflicts.

Will Ryan recognise that his actions are controlling and address his trust issues, or will Megan decide that the relationship is becoming too suffocating to continue?

Scenario 4

Keira and Timothy have been together for several months. Keira begins to criticise Timothy's appearance and clothing choices, making him feel self-conscious. He wonders if he should change his sense of style to please Keira, or if he should stand up for himself.

Will Timothy confront Keira about her controlling behaviour, or will he decide that a partner who truly cares for him would accept him as he is?

If you are in an abusive relationship, or know anyone else who might be, here are some tips for getting help:

- **Talk to someone:** Talk to someone you trust about what's going on and let them know your concerns. Ask them to support you or go with you to the Gardaí, if that's what you want to do.
- **Contact a helpline:**
    - Text SPUNOUT to 50808
    - Call Women's Aid on 1800 341 900
    - Call Childline on 1800 66 66 66
    - Call Men's Aid on 01 554 3811
    - Call Samaritans on 116 123 or email jo@samaritans.ie
- **Seek support organisations and emergency accommodation:** SAFE Ireland provides contact details for specialist domestic violence services across Ireland. AMEN is a voluntary group that provides a confidential helpline, information and a support service for male victims of domestic abuse and their children.
- **See a counsellor:** Seeing a counsellor or a domestic violence support worker can help you work through your feelings and rebuild your confidence.
- **See these websites for additional support:**
    - Spunout.ie
    - Safeireland.ie
    - Text50808.ie
    - Barnardos.ie
    - Womensaid.ie
    - Mensaid.ie
    - Toointoyou.ie

ACTIVITY 26.4 – CREATE

In groups, choose one of the websites in the Top Tips box above that offers support and advice for victims of abuse and coercive control. Research the organisation and create a digital presentation to show other students what services are offered by the organisation.

How to end a relationship respectfully

Many people struggle to end their relationships. This may be because they are unsure of how to do it, or they feel guilty about doing so. Sometimes, people will even stay in a relationship for longer than necessary because they fear the consequences of ending it.

Ending a romantic relationship is a difficult and emotionally challenging process. The decision to do it takes careful consideration, and people must take responsibility for their choice.

Here are some guidelines on how to respectfully end a relationship:

1. Decide that the relationship is over

To drift along in a relationship that's no longer satisfying and fulfilling could cause you more harm than good. If you consistently feel unhappy, unfulfilled or unsupported in your relationship, then it's likely time for the relationship to end. The decision to end a relationship will usually happen when all efforts to communicate and resolve issues have failed.

2. End the relationship in person

A face-to-face conversation in a quiet space is essential. Meeting to say 'goodbye' to the relationship you shared is respectful, considerate and compassionate. Ending a relationship by text or voice message is impersonal and does not allow both people to have their say.

3. Be truthful and honest

Be honest about why the relationship no longer works for you. Let the other person know what led you to this decision, without going back over every single incident. Don't resort to blaming the other person or being critical. This conversation is for closure – avoid getting into an argument, even if you're provoked.

4. Allow the other person to express their feelings in a healthy manner

Whatever your concerns are, the other person deserves the chance to express their feelings as well. By listening to them, you show them that you care about them as a person, even if you no longer want a relationship with them.

5. Prepare to cut all ties

After you have had the break-up conversation, it's advisable to stop communicating for a while. This will allow you to process the ending of the relationship and your feelings about it. Ending a meaningful relationship can feel like a loss, so it's important to look after your wellbeing. It's sometimes possible to maintain a friendship after a break-up, but this depends on the situation.

ACTIVITY 26.5 – ROLE PLAY

A. In pairs, role play one of the scenarios below. One person should take on the role of ending the relationship, and the other should react to the news. Use the guidelines for ending a relationship respectfully to help you.

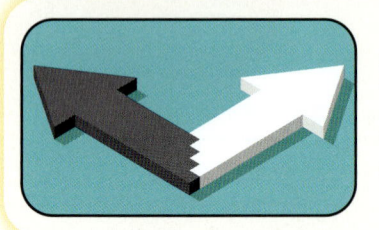

Scenario 1
As a couple, you have grown apart over time. One of you has decided to end the relationship now.

Scenario 2
One of you is moving to a different county for college. You don't want a long-distance relationship, so you have decided to end the relationship.

Scenario 3
You have noticed that your partner is becoming more and more controlling of you. You don't think this behaviour is a sign of a healthy relationship, so you have decided to end it.

B. Reflection questions:
1. How did it feel to play the role of the person ending the relationship?
2. How did it feel to be on the receiving end of the bad news?
3. What were the challenges of ending the relationship respectfully?
4. What strategies or communication techniques did you use to make the break-up as respectful as possible?

The emotional impact of ending relationships

Ending relationships can be very hard, especially for teenagers, who are still learning how to process intense emotions and feelings. When ending relationships, teenagers often:

- feel sad, angry and emotionally drained, and may cry a lot
- don't want to hang out with friends
- struggle with schoolwork
- start questioning if they're good enough or if they're likeable
- find it hard to trust people again.

It's normal for teenagers to be mad at their ex-partner or even at themselves for things they think they did wrong. They may feel lonely or isolated if they share friends with their ex-partner and can no longer be around them. It can also feel awkward to bump into an ex-partner. Sometimes, teenagers jump into a new relationship quickly to try to feel better, but this can have its own problems.

However, ending relationships can also have positive impacts for teenagers:
- They learn to be more resilient.
- They understand what they really want and need in a relationship.
- They get to know themselves better.
- They feel more confident just being themselves.
- They might find new things they like to do.
- They become closer with other friends.

ACTIVITY 26.6 – THINK

In this activity, you will work together to create a Resilience Tree.

A. Your teacher will draw the outline of a tree on the board. Identify the different emotions and feelings a person may experience when ending a relationship, and write these down on a Post-it note. When instructed, stick your notes on the board to represent the leaves of the tree.

B. On a separate Post-it note, write down the coping tools a person could use to help them get through the ending of a relationship. Stick your notes around the roots of the tree. The roots represent resilience – they are the anchors that keep us grounded when times are tough.

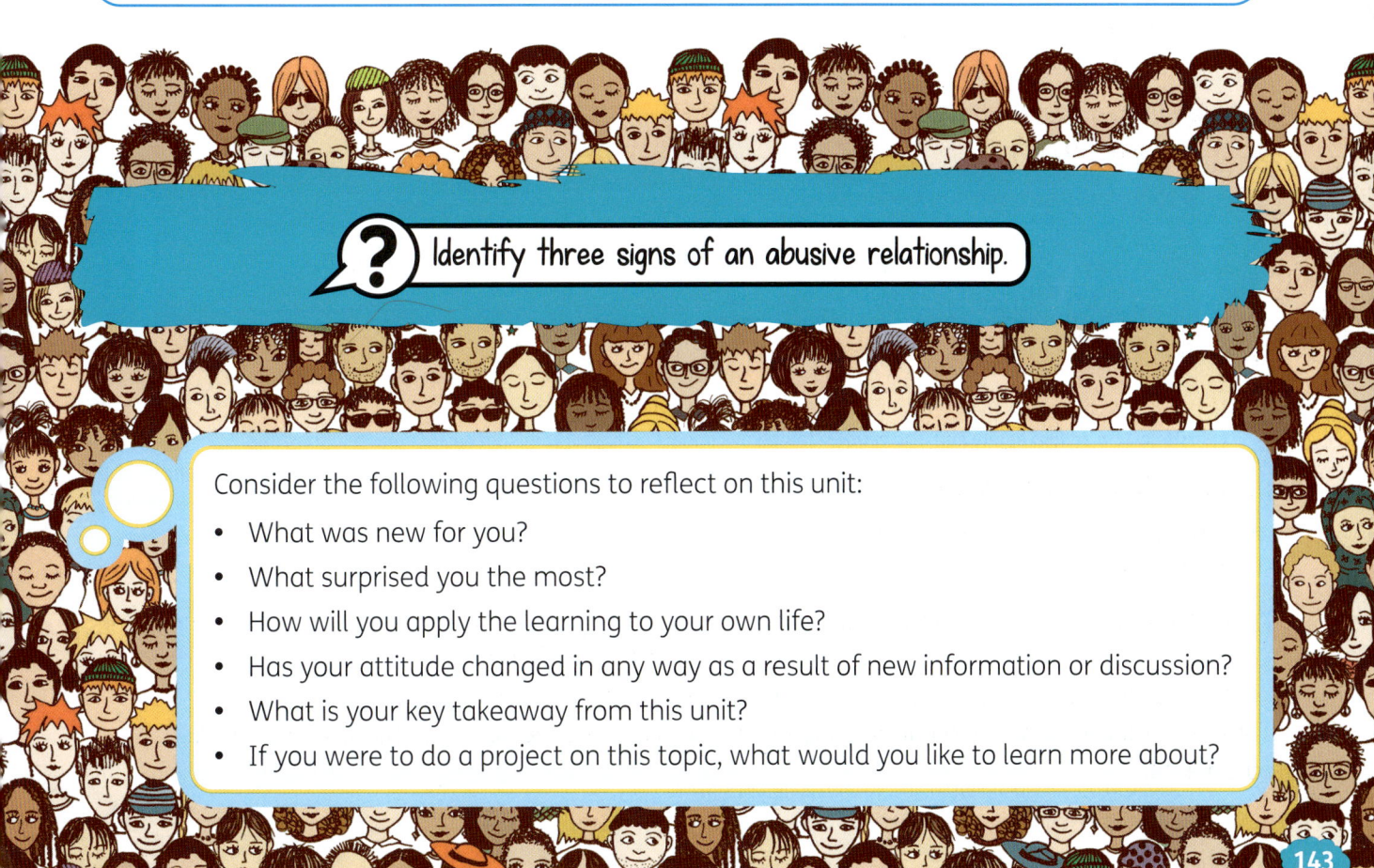

? Identify three signs of an abusive relationship.

Consider the following questions to reflect on this unit:
- What was new for you?
- What surprised you the most?
- How will you apply the learning to your own life?
- Has your attitude changed in any way as a result of new information or discussion?
- What is your key takeaway from this unit?
- If you were to do a project on this topic, what would you like to learn more about?

UNIT OF LEARNING 5

Sexual and Emotional Wellbeing

The chapters in this Unit of Learning are:
- Chapter 27 – Sexual Harassment
- Chapter 28 – The Influence of Social Media on Gender Norms
- Chapter 29 – Contraception: Options and Communication
- Chapter 30 – Contraception: Making Choices
- Chapter 31 – STIs: Transmission and Types
- Chapter 32 – STIs: Testing and Treatment

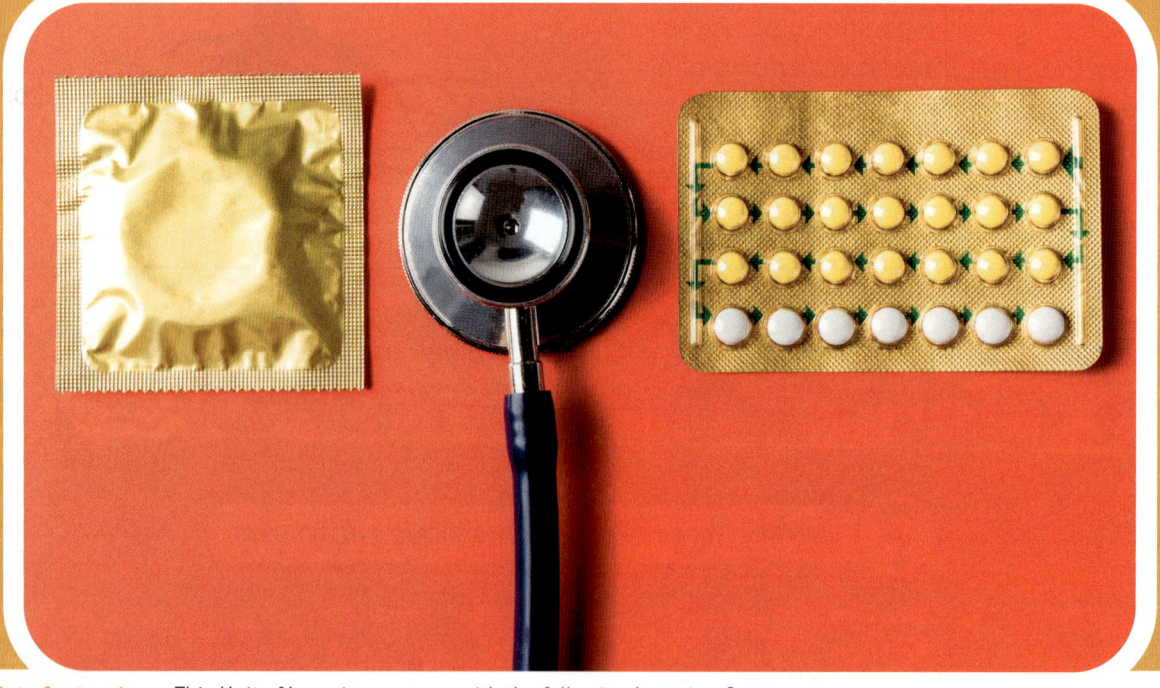

Note for teachers: This Unit of Learning engages with the following Learning Outcomes:

- **1.5** reflect on gender equity and how gender stereotypes impact on expectations, behaviour and relationships
- **3.1** reflect on the values, behaviours and skills that help to make, sustain and end relationships respectfully with friends, family and romantic/intimate relationships
- **3.3** identify signs of healthy, unhealthy and abusive relationships
- **3.5** consider the importance of taking care of their reproductive health
- **3.9** explain the importance of safer sexual activity with reference to methods of contraception and protection against sexually transmitted infections (STIs)
- **3.10** discuss the influence of popular culture and the online world, in particular, the influence of pornography, on young people's understanding, expectations and social norms in relation to sexual expression
- **3.11** demonstrate how to access and appraise appropriate and trustworthy advice, support and services related to relationships and sexual health
- **4.9** demonstrate how to access and appraise appropriate and trustworthy information and services aimed at supporting young people's emotional wellbeing and mental health

Related Learning Outcomes: 3.1, 3.3, 3.11.

CHAPTER 27

Sexual Harassment

In this chapter we will:
- define harassment and explore different types of it
- learn about sexual harassment
- consider the barriers to seeking help for harassment.

KEY TERMS
Harassment
Sexual harassment
Sexual assault
Sexual coercion

? Why is it important to respect people's physical and sexual boundaries?

Harassment

Harassment is repeated unwanted behaviour that offends someone or makes them feel distressed, disturbed, annoyed or intimidated. This behaviour can be verbal, written, physical or digital, and may target people based on their:
- race
- ethnicity
- religion
- disability
- sexual orientation
- gender.

Types of harassment include:

Verbal harassment
This involves using offensive language, making threats, or name-calling to insult someone.

Physical harassment
This includes any form of physical aggression or unwanted touching that violates someone's personal space and makes them feel uncomfortable or threatened.

Cyberbullying
This is harassment carried out using digital means, such as on social media or online forums, or through instant messaging or emails.

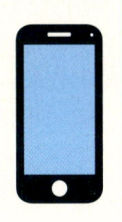

Workplace harassment
This is negative behaviour that occurs within a professional environment. This behaviour impacts an employee's work performance and creates a toxic work environment.

Stalking
This is a pattern of unwanted, fixated and obsessive behaviour that causes serious alarm, distress or fear of violence. Stalking behaviour includes:
- following a person around
- obsessively monitoring a person's activity, both in person and online
- attempting to contact a person by any means.

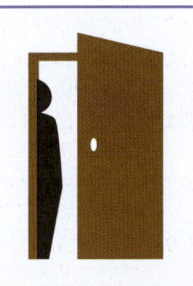

145

Sexual harassment

Sexual harassment is when a person makes unwanted sexual advances towards another person. It can include:
- unwanted touching and physical contact
- making promises in return for sexual acts
- leering and staring
- sexual gestures and body movements
- comments of a sexual nature
- sending unwanted images of a sexual nature
- questions about a person's sex life
- sex-based insults
- displaying rude and offensive material, such as pornographic or explicit images
- rude phone calls
- indecent exposure (a person deliberately revealing their genitals).

Sexual assault and sexual coercion are also forms of sexual harassment:

> **Sexual assault** refers to any sexual act that a person did not consent to or is forced into against their will. Rape is a type of sexual assault, and involves forced penetration of the vagina, anus or mouth. Groping, forced kissing and sexual acts with a minor are also types of sexual assault.

> **Sexual coercion** refers to unwanted sexual activity that a person is pressured into through non-physical means. It often happens in abusive relationships, and can involve:
> - repeated requests for sexual activity
> - the use of guilt or shame to pressure a person into engaging in an activity (e.g. saying, 'You would do it if you loved me.')
> - threats to end the relationship if a person does not engage in sexual activity
> - emotional blackmail
> - threats to a person's children, home or job
> - threats to lie about or spread rumours about the person.

Harassment and the law

There are laws in Ireland that protect people against harassment:

Harassment, Harmful Communications and Related Offences Act 2020 (Coco's Law)
- This law outlaws the sharing of, or threatening to share, intimate images of a person without their consent, with or without intent to cause harm to that person.
- It prohibits intentionally causing harm to another person by sending a threatening or very offensive message either to them or about them online.
- There are strong penalties for these offences, including up to ten years' imprisonment and large fines.

Employment Equality Acts 1998–2015
Under these acts, sexual harassment and harassment of an employee in the workplace are against the law.

CHAPTER 27 – SEXUAL HARASSMENT

If you experience any behaviour of a sexual nature that is unwanted and makes you feel uncomfortable, this is sexual harassment. You do not have to tolerate it. If it takes place at work or while you are using a service (e.g. a café, library, concert or hospital), your employer or the service provider is required by law to protect you from sexual harassment. If it takes place at school, inform an adult working in the school such as a year head, a teacher, the guidance counsellor or the principal.

ACTIVITY 27.1 – THINK

In pairs, indicate whether you think the behaviours below are examples of harassment or not.

	Behaviour	Harassment	Not harassment
1	Sending abusive messages to someone after they 'ghost' you (cut off all communication without explanation) following a date.		
2	Repeatedly checking a person's social media accounts to find out where they are and where they are going, in the hopes of bumping into them.		
3	Getting upset when your partner says they want to end the relationship.		
4	Telling your ex that you miss them, in the presence of your shared friendship group.		
5	Sending abusive messages to your ex's new partner.		
6	Snooping on a classmate's laptop to get more information about them.		
7	Turning up to school or work with flowers every day for a week in the hope of changing someone's mind about dating you.		
8	Going to your ex's home to talk, and switching between compliments and insults when they don't agree to try the relationship again.		
9	Threatening to post sexually explicit photos of your partner as revenge for ending the relationship.		
10	Ringing your ex several times using friends' phones after they said they did not want to hear from you and blocked your number.		
11	Trying to apologise or win someone back by ringing them once or twice.		

ACTIVITY 27.2 – WATCH

Watch this video about an incident of sexual harassment and answer the questions that follow.

▶ www.educate*plus*.ie/go/sexual-harassment

1. Do you think Kim is a good friend to Willow?
2. Why did Willow feel uncomfortable at the party?
3. How did Willow feel when the boy started to kiss and touch her?
4. Did he respect her wishes?
5. What did Willow decide to do?
6. How did Willow feel when she was taken advantage of?
7. How did Kim feel in the end?
8. How can bystanders, such as Kim, play a role in preventing situations from escalating into sexual harassment?
9. In your opinion, could Willow have handled things differently at any point?

TIPS

Here are some safety tips for dealing with harassment:

- If someone's behaviour makes you uncomfortable in any way, listen to your instincts and take action immediately.
- When turning someone down, be very clear about your decision.
- Don't try to be gentle with someone who makes you feel uncomfortable – this could be misinterpreted as giving mixed signals. Use assertive communication: communicate respectfully but firmly, making sure to stand up for your rights and personal boundaries.
- Cut off all contact with someone if you don't feel comfortable seeing them again.
- Tell people you trust about what is happening to you. They can offer valuable advice and support.
- Don't hesitate to seek help at school (teachers, year head, guidance counsellor), from the Gardaí or from organisations such the Rape Crisis Centre.
- Be cyber secure: change passwords, check privacy settings and scan for spyware.

ACTIVITY 27.3 – DISCUSS

A. If someone is being sexually harassed, what might be the barriers to seeking help? In groups, brainstorm answers to this question.

B. Discuss your answers as a class.

CHAPTER 27 – SEXUAL HARASSMENT

ACTIVITY 27.4 – READ

In groups, read this case study and answer the questions that follow.

Case study

Grace is 16 and is about to start Transition Year. Recently, she joined a new sports team and was excited about the opportunity to make new friends. However, soon after joining, she started experiencing uncomfortable incidents with one of her teammates, Matthew. Matthew, also 16, began making inappropriate comments about Grace's appearance. He also began making unwelcome advances towards her during training sessions.

Initially, Grace was unsure about how to handle the situation. She didn't want to cause any trouble or risk being isolated by her teammates, so she didn't speak up about what was happening. However, the constant harassment began to affect her emotional wellbeing and her performance on the team. She decided to confide in her best friend, Susan, about what was happening.

1. Is Matthew's behaviour appropriate?
2. Why was Grace hesitant to say anything in the beginning?
3. How would you define what is happening to Grace?
4. What are some common forms of sexual harassment that teenagers might experience?
5. Where could Grace report instances of sexual harassment?

ACTIVITY 27.5 – CREATE

CBA 2

In groups, design a campaign to create awareness about sexual harassment. For your campaign, create a pamphlet that includes the following information:

- definitions and types of harassment, with a focus on sexual harassment
- behaviours that constitute sexual harassment
- the emotional and legal consequences of sexual harassment
- tips for dealing with harassment
- resources to teach people more about sexual harassment, including how and where to get help.

Use information, statistics and research from reliable websites, and present your findings in a visually engaging way (e.g. graphs, tables, infographics).

? What role does assertive communication play in stopping harassment?

Related Learning Outcomes: 1.5, 3.10, 4.9.

CHAPTER 28

The Influence of Social Media on Gender Norms

In this chapter we will:
- examine what gender norms are
- explore how social media can influence gender norms
- identify types of negative social media influencers
- discuss how to be a critical consumer of social media content.

KEY TERMS
Norms
Gender norms
Socialisation
Misogynist
Critical consumer

❓ On a scale of 1 to 5, how much influence do you think social media has on us?

What are gender norms?

Norms are the commonly accepted and expected behaviours, rules and standards within a specific group or society. An example of a norm in Ireland is greeting people with a friendly 'Hello'.

Gender norms are roles and expectations that society assigns to people based on their perceived gender identity. These norms are rules that dictate how men and women are expected to behave, dress and interact within society. Gender norms can be harmful and have a negative impact on people personally and professionally.

Examples of gender norms include:

> The expectation that women should take on more nurturing and caregiving roles in society.

> The expectation that men should take on roles that emphasise strength and leadership.

Gender norms are often reinforced through **socialisation** (the process of learning behaviours from other people), media representations and cultural traditions. For example:

Girls may be encouraged to play with dolls, learn homemaking skills, and prioritise empathy and emotional expression. As they mature, they may be encouraged to pursue careers in fields like nursing, teaching or social work, which are traditionally associated with caregiving roles.	Boys may be encouraged to play with trucks and action figures, learn practical skills such as fixing things, and display assertiveness and strength. As they mature, they may be encouraged to pursue careers in fields like engineering, politics or business, which are traditionally associated with leadership and authority.

Gender norms are socially constructed (created by people in society) and vary greatly across different cultures and time periods. Challenging and breaking down harmful gender norms helps to promote gender equality and create a more inclusive society.

ACTIVITY 28.1 – DISCUSS

In groups, brainstorm and make a list of gender norms that you believe exist in Irish society. For example:
- The expectation that men are primarily responsible for physically demanding jobs.
- The expectation that women are primarily responsible for looking after the house and the family.

Share your lists with the class and engage in a class discussion about the topic.

Gender norms and social media

There is a vast amount of content shared and consumed on social media every day. People can be influenced by the images, messages and behaviours they see and witness online, often unconsciously. Gender-related ideas and gender norms are often promoted and reinforced on social media platforms.

Here are some of the impacts of social media on gender norms:

1. Representation
Social media can often reinforce traditional gender norms, but it can also challenge them by representing diverse gender identities and expressions. For example: showcasing empowered women in leadership roles.

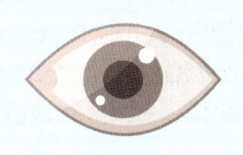

2. Cyberbullying and harassment
Social media can reinforce harmful stereotypes and gender-based harassment, as some users may face online abuse due to their gender identity or expression.

3. Creating echo chambers
Social media algorithms are rules that decide what users see based on their past online behaviour. These algorithms can reinforce gender norms by showing users content that aligns with their pre-existing beliefs. This creates an echo chamber where the same content is repeatedly circulated back to a person, without any opposing or differing viewpoints to challenge it.

4. Providing a platform
Social media provides a platform for gender activists and allies to raise awareness, advocate for gender equality and challenge harmful gender norms. It can also provide a platform for those who want to reinforce harmful gender norms.

Overall, the impact of social media on gender norms can be both positive and negative, depending on how users engage with and respond to the content they encounter.

ACTIVITY 28.2 – THINK
As a class, brainstorm a list of online influencers that you follow on social media. Discuss why you follow these influencers.

Negative social media influencers

Negative social media influencers are people who use their online presence to:
- promote harmful behaviours
- spread misinformation
- reinforce toxic ideas.

They often have a large following and can influence the thoughts, attitudes and actions of their audience in harmful ways. Here are some types of negative influencers on social media:

Promoters of harmful gender norms
Some influencers, often those with a large social media following, may use their platform to sustain certain gender norms and actions that can be harmful.

Promoters of unhealthy body image
Some influencers promote unrealistic beauty standards and body ideals, leading to body shaming, eating disorders and low self-esteem among their followers.

Cyberbullies and trolls
Certain influencers engage in cyberbullying and online harassment, targeting individuals or groups with hurtful comments, threats or harmful content.

Advocates of dangerous behaviours
Some influencers may glorify risky behaviours like substance abuse, reckless driving or self-harm, encouraging their followers to engage in potentially harmful activities.

Spreaders of misinformation
Influencers who share false information, conspiracy theories or unverified claims can mislead their followers, leading to a lack of trust in reliable sources and potential harm to public health and safety.

Encouragers of hate speech
Negative influencers who promote hate speech, racism, sexism or other forms of discrimination contribute to a toxic online environment. They can create and encourage hostility and division among their audience.

Scammers and fraudsters
Some influencers may use their platform to promote fraudulent schemes, products or services, exploiting their followers' trust for personal gain.

Conflict instigators
Certain influencers thrive on creating drama, starting online conflicts and encouraging negative interactions among their followers.

CHAPTER 28 – THE INFLUENCE OF SOCIAL MEDIA ON GENDER NORMS

ACTIVITY 28.3 – READ

In groups, read these online comments from social media influencers and answer the questions that follow.

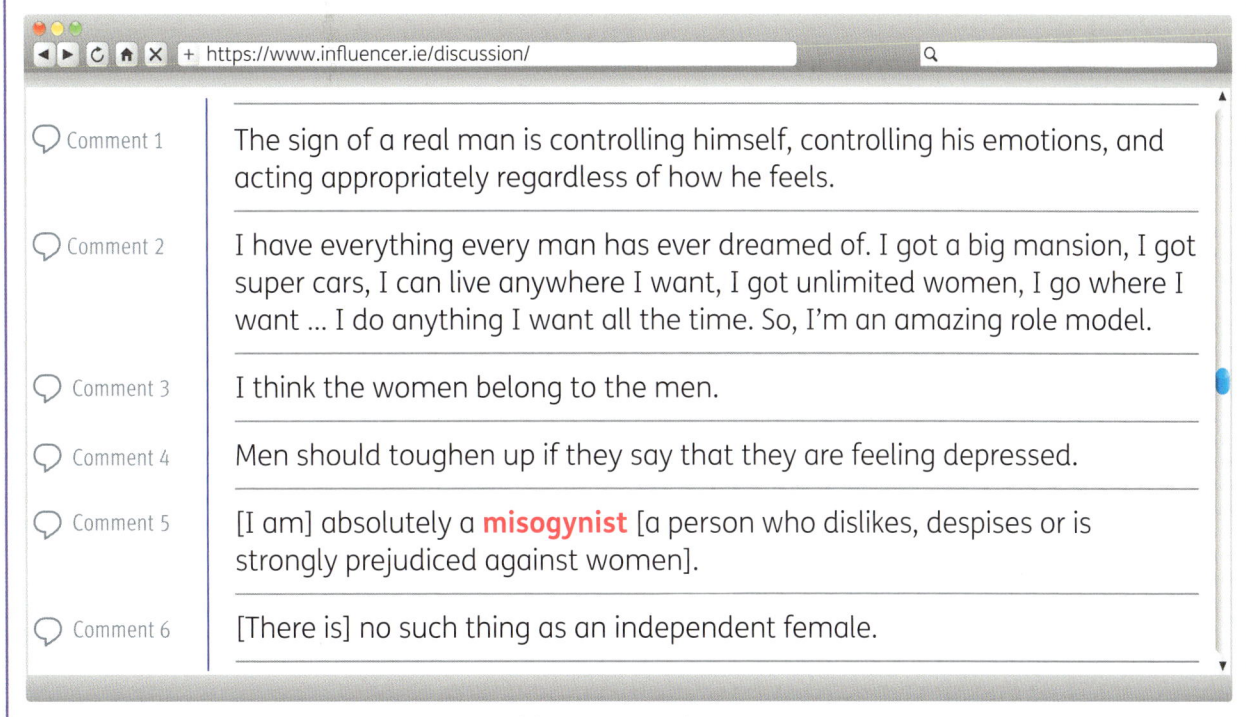

https://www.influencer.ie/discussion/

Comment 1	The sign of a real man is controlling himself, controlling his emotions, and acting appropriately regardless of how he feels.
Comment 2	I have everything every man has ever dreamed of. I got a big mansion, I got super cars, I can live anywhere I want, I got unlimited women, I go where I want … I do anything I want all the time. So, I'm an amazing role model.
Comment 3	I think the women belong to the men.
Comment 4	Men should toughen up if they say that they are feeling depressed.
Comment 5	[I am] absolutely a **misogynist** [a person who dislikes, despises or is strongly prejudiced against women].
Comment 6	[There is] no such thing as an independent female.

1. Overall, are these comments positive or negative?
2. What message does each comment send out?
3. What gender roles and norms do these comments set for men and women?
4. What influence could these comments have on people's beliefs, behaviours and wellbeing?
5. What might be the consequences of spreading these messages?

ACTIVITY 28.4 – READ

In groups, read this case study and answer the questions that follow.

Case study

Gemma, Ria, Joey and Rory are four teenagers who are active social media users. They have been friends for years and know each other well. However, they've started noticing that their views on gender norms and self-expression have changed since they were children.

Gemma and Ria have been following several popular fashion influencers on TikTok who often promote ideas of the 'perfect woman'. According to them, women should wear certain clothes, use specific beauty products and look a certain way in order to be desirable and successful. Gemma and Ria feel pressured to conform to these standards, and often compare themselves to these influencers. As a result, they both have low self-esteem and body insecurities.

153

Meanwhile, Joey and Rory have been watching YouTube videos by male gamers and fitness enthusiasts who project their ideas of the 'perfect man'. For example, they believe men should have a certain build, treat people a certain way and not express their emotions. As a result, Joey and Rory have started working out more and acting 'tough' when they communicate with others online. They have also started avoiding activities they consider to be 'feminine'.

Because of these social media influences, the dynamics within the friend group have also changed. Gemma, who used to enjoy playing sports with the boys, now hesitates to join them out of fear of being 'unfeminine'. Joey, who used to be open about his emotions, now suppresses (ignores) them to seem more masculine.

1. How has social media influenced the teenagers' awareness and understanding of gender norms?
2. What specific content has contributed to the changes in the teenagers' behaviour?
3. How are Gemma and Ria affected differently by social media influences compared to Joey and Rory?
4. Discuss the potential long-term effects of these social media influences on the four teenagers.
5. How does social media keep harmful gender norms and stereotypes alive?
6. In what ways can social media help to challenge traditional gender norms and promote gender equality?

Being a critical consumer of social media content

A **critical consumer** is someone who is thoughtful about the things they receive or buy, such as messages, news, products or services. Being a critical consumer of social media content involves being mindful of the information you encounter online. This allows you to navigate social media responsibly, and helps to create a more informed and balanced digital community.

By applying these strategies, you can develop the skills to be a critical consumer:

1. Verify the source
Always check the credibility and reliability of the sources behind the content. Look for content from experts, well-known organisations or verified accounts.

2. Question the intent
Consider the motivation or agenda behind the content. Ask yourself why the information is being shared and if there might be biases or more sinister motives.

CHAPTER 28 – THE INFLUENCE OF SOCIAL MEDIA ON GENDER NORMS

3. Cross check information
Don't rely solely on one source. Verify information using multiple perspectives and compare data from different sources.

4. Fact check information
Look for fact-checking resources or use fact-checking websites to verify the accuracy of claims and statements.

5. Recognise misinformation
Look out for misinformation, false news or conspiracy theories. Learn to identify common patterns and warning signs.

6. Evaluate the tone and language
Pay attention to the tone and language used in the content. Be cautious of 'clickbait' headlines and emotionally manipulative content.

7. Be mindful of algorithms
Social media algorithms personalise content based on your previous interactions and activity. Be aware of how this can create echo chambers, and actively seek out diverse content.

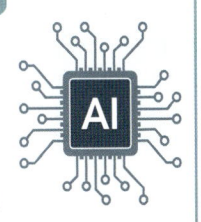

8. Reflect on emotional responses
Be aware of your emotional reactions to content. Take a step back before sharing or reacting impulsively to something, to ensure you're not contributing to the spread of misinformation.

9. Question images and videos
Be critical of images and videos shared online. They can be easily edited or taken out of context.

10. Protect your privacy
Be cautious about sharing personal information online. Regularly review your privacy settings on social media platforms.

ACTIVITY 28.5 – CREATE
CBA 1

In groups, identify and research positive social media influencers who promote inclusivity, diversity and healthy values. Create a digital presentation on the influencer you have chosen and share it with the class.

> **?** Identify two strategies that can be used to question negative gender norms on social media.

Related Learning Outcomes: 3.5, 3.9.

CHAPTER 29

Contraception: Options and Communication

In this chapter we will:
- consider how contraception leads to safer sexual activity
- explore contraception options
- examine facts about contraception and young people in Ireland
- explain the importance of communicating about contraception.

? What is contraception used for?

KEY TERMS
Dual protection

Contraception and safer sexual activity

Safer sexual activity involves using contraception to protect against unplanned pregnancies and sexually transmitted infections (STIs). It allows people to make informed choices about their sexual and reproductive health. If a person is sexually active, they are at risk of contracting an STI regardless of their sexual orientation or gender.

ACTIVITY 29.1 – THINK

Can you remember any of the hormonal and non-hormonal (barrier) methods of contraception that we learned about in Second Year? In pairs, fill in the table below in your copies with as many methods as you can remember. List any other methods that you are aware of.

Hormonal	Non-hormonal (barrier)

Contraception options

Safer sexual activity involves a person choosing the contraception option that best suits their situation and lifestyle. Certain contraceptives better suit certain people for a variety of reasons. It's advisable to talk to a GP about what type of contraception would be best. When used correctly and consistently, the majority of contraception options are highly effective.

Some people might decide to use only short-term contraceptives (e.g. condoms), while others may choose a long-term contraceptive such as an implant or an injection. This will depend on people's preferences. For example, some people believe that long-term methods are more reliable and protective.

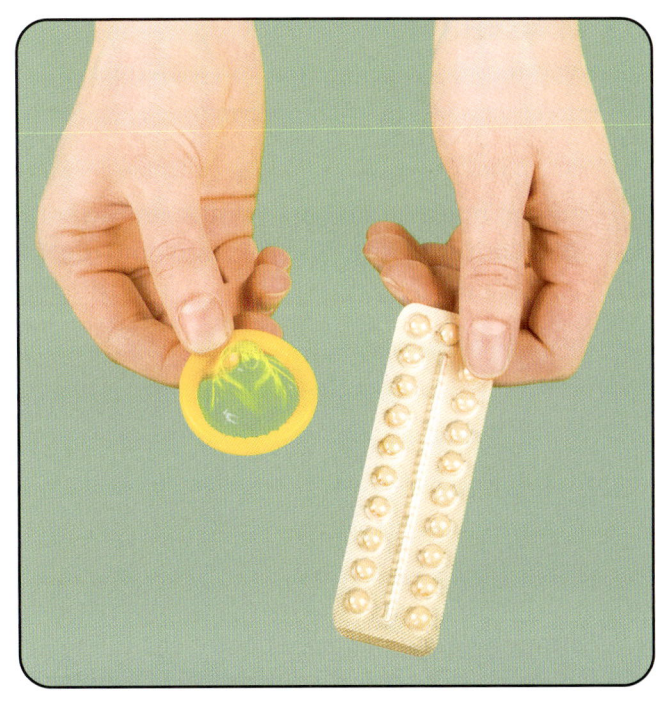

Using **dual protection** (both condoms and another method of contraception, such as the pill) allows people to have safer sex, as it offers the best protection against pregnancy and STIs.

ACTIVITY 29.2 – CREATE

A. In groups, you will be assigned one of the following contraception methods:

- Combined oral contraception (the pill)
- The copper coil (IUD)
- The implant
- Intrauterine system (IUS)
- The mini pill
- Male condom
- Female condom
- Injectable contraception
- The patch
- Vaginal ring
- The diaphragm (the cap)
- Sterilisation

Research your assigned contraception method on this website:
www.educate*plus*.ie/go/contraception-methods

Based on your research, create a six-slide presentation using a software of your choice (PowerPoint, Prezi, Google Slides, etc.). Your presentation should include the following headings:

- Type of contraception (hormonal or non-hormonal)
- How does it work?
- How effective is it?
- Advantages
- Disadvantages
- Considerations before using it

Include text and images in the presentation.

B. Present your presentation to the class.

Facts about contraception and young people in Ireland

According to recent research:

33% of young people reported having had sexual intercourse by the age of 17.

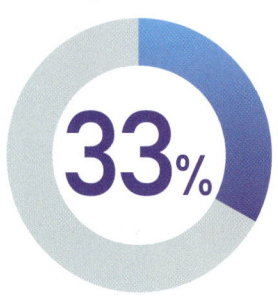

Almost 90% of young people who have had sexual intercourse said that they used contraception when first having sex.

Nearly a quarter of young people who have had sexual intercourse expressed regret over the timing of their first sexual experience.

25% expressed regret

Among young people who are sexually active, just under 80% reported 'always' using contraception. 56% reported using a condom 'all the time':

Category	%
Overall	55.9
Male	59.0
Female	52.5
Age 16/17	56.7
Age 18	53.8
5th year	56.8
6th year	57.7
Left school	51.3

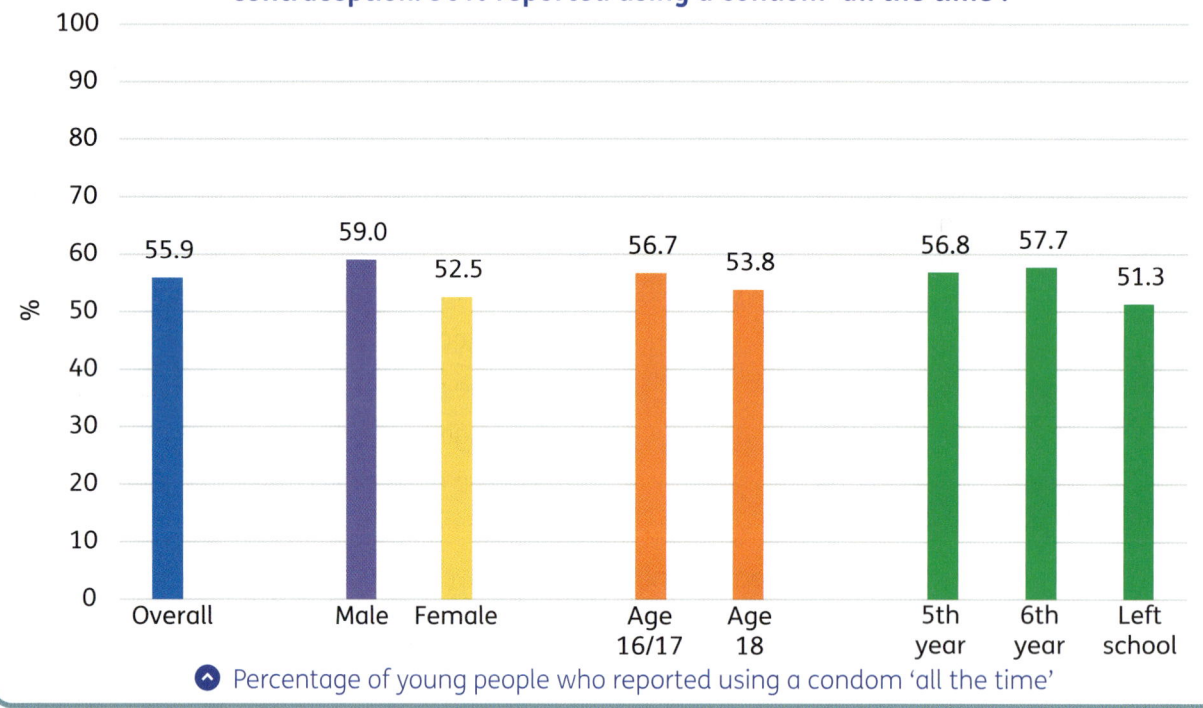

Percentage of young people who reported using a condom 'all the time'

ACTIVITY 29.3 – THINK

Answer these questions based on the facts about contraception and young people in Ireland above.

1. Almost 90 per cent of young people who have had sexual intercourse said that they used contraception when first having sex. What could be the risks for the other ten per cent of young people?
2. Why, in your opinion, would some young people express regret over the timing of their first sexual experience?
3. Fifty-six per cent of people reported using a condom 'all the time'. Why might using a condom offer good protection?

CHAPTER 29 – CONTRACEPTION: OPTIONS AND COMMUNICATION

Communicating about contraception

Contraception should be discussed by anyone who is thinking about becoming sexually active, regardless of sexual orientation or gender. When couples choose to engage in sexual activity, it's very important that they communicate about contraception beforehand. This increases the safety of the sexual activity.

Sharing the responsibility of protection from the start can prevent unwanted consequences and also build a healthy relationship. Though it might be challenging, it's crucial for people to openly discuss and negotiate the use of contraception. Here is some advice on how people can communicate about contraception:

- **Practise what they want to say:** Rehearsing the words out loud beforehand can help the conversation feel smoother, especially if nerves get in the way. People can practise saying the words in front of a mirror a few times. It's important to be clear about what they want.
- **Turn to someone they trust:** Asking a friend to rehearse the conversation can help it seem less daunting.
- **Time and place:** Pick a time and place to discuss contraception, ensuring that the environment is as stress-free as possible for both partners.

ACTIVITY 29.4 – READ

Read this case study and answer the questions that follow.

Case study

Linda (18) and Ivan (19) have been in an intimate relationship for a few months. They were friends first and always got on really well. Before they started to be sexually active, Ivan told Linda that she should go on the pill, as he decided that the pill would be the best option for both of them. Linda wasn't sure about this, but she went along with Ivan's suggestion. She spoke to her GP, who prescribed her the pill.

Since getting the pill, Linda has forgotten to take it on a number of occasions. She has also noticed that she has been quite moody since she started taking it. She is worried about discussing this with Ivan or anyone else because she finds the whole topic of contraception very awkward.

1. Do you think that this couple is well protected by Linda taking the pill?
2. Do you think that Linda and Ivan effectively communicated about contraception before becoming sexually active?
3. Why do you think that Linda went along with Ivan's suggestion?
4. Why do you think that Ivan decided that Linda should go on the pill?
5. How could both partners have communicated more effectively?
6. What should Linda do now?
7. What should Ivan do now?

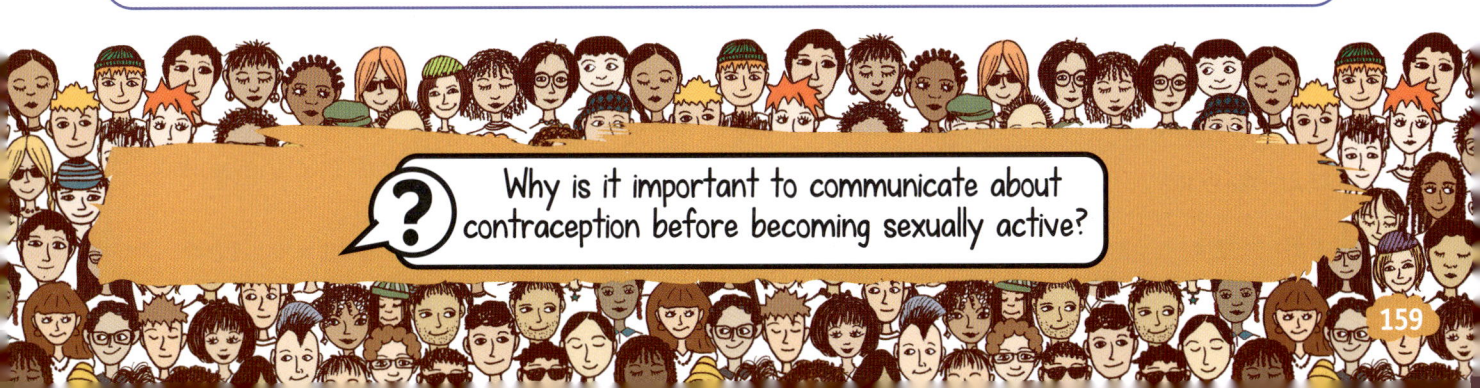

> **?** Why is it important to communicate about contraception before becoming sexually active?

Related Learning Outcomes: 3.5, 3.9.

CHAPTER 30

Contraception: Making Choices

In this chapter we will:
- explore the history of contraception in Ireland
- examine the factors that affect our contraception choices
- learn how to use a condom correctly.

KEY TERMS
Condoms
Withdrawal method

? What must a person consider when choosing a contraceptive?

ACTIVITY 30.1 – THINK

To familiarise yourself with the range of contraceptive choices available, match these contraceptives to their correct description.

	Contraceptive		Description
1	Female condom	A	A small, T-shaped plastic frame with copper wire that is placed in the woman's womb to prevent sperm from reaching and combining with the egg.
2	The mini pill	B	A surgical procedure to provide permanent contraception.
3	Male condom	C	A progestogen-only pill that contains no oestrogen.
4	Combined oral contraception (the pill)	D	A small, flexible ring that is placed in the vagina.
5	The copper coil	E	A tablet that contains artificial versions of the two female hormones, oestrogen and progesterone.
6	The implant	F	A soft silicone device that is put into the vagina to cover the cervix (neck of the womb).
7	Intrauterine system (IUS)	G	A patch placed on a woman's skin that releases hormones.
8	Vaginal ring	H	A type of barrier method that is placed into a woman's vagina before sex to help prevent pregnancy and STIs.
9	The diaphragm (the cap)	I	An artificial form of the hormone progesterone that is injected into the woman's arm or buttocks.
10	Injectable contraception	J	A small, flexible rod that is put under the skin of a woman's upper arm.
11	Sterilisation	K	A type of barrier method that is placed over a man's penis before sex to help prevent a woman becoming pregnant and to prevent the spread of STIs.
12	The patch	L	A small, T-shaped plastic device that is put into the womb to prevent pregnancy.

1 = ___ 2 = ___ 3 = ___ 4 = ___ 5 = ___ 6 = ___ 7 = ___ 8 = ___ 9 = ___ 10 = ___ 11 = ___ 12 = ___

The history of contraception in Ireland

Contraception was not always legal or widely available in Ireland due to social and religious reasons. The strong influence of the Catholic Church affected people's abilities to prevent or plan for pregnancies. It opposed most methods of contraception due to the belief that the main purpose of sexual intercourse is for married couples to have children. Here is an overview of Ireland's history of and journey towards access to contraception:

1935: Contraception was made illegal in Ireland.

1946: The government banned books about family planning and contraceptives. Lack of sex education in schools further led to a lack of understanding of reproductive health.

1960s–1970s: Despite the illegal status of the contraceptive pill, it was sometimes prescribed by doctors to help regulate women's periods. However, access remained limited.

1974: The McGee case was a legal breakthrough that recognised couples' right to privacy when planning their families.

1970s–1990s: Feminist groups protested and advocated for easier access to contraception. Gradual changes to the law saw condoms and other contraceptives become legal and more readily available.

Today: Contraception is now free for individuals aged 17 to 25. However, certain barriers to contraception, such as cost, remain a factor for other groups.

Factors that affect our contraception choices

A person must evaluate the pros and cons of each form of contraception with a GP to decide whether it's suitable for them. This will give them the greatest protection against STIs and unplanned pregnancy. The factors to consider include:

- how effective it is
- potential side effects
- how frequently it needs to be taken or replaced
- how easy it is to use
- the cost.

Other factors that can affect a person's choice include:
- **Health issues:** A person might have a medical condition that prevents them from using a certain form of contraception.
- **Lifestyle factors:** A single person's contraceptive needs might be different from someone in a relationship.
- **Beliefs and values:** A person's beliefs and values could prevent them from using different forms of contraception.

ACTIVITY 30.2 – DISCUSS

A. In groups, research and brainstorm other factors that a person might consider when choosing methods of contraception. List these factors under the following headings:
- Health issues
- Lifestyle factors
- Beliefs and values

B. Your teacher will put some poster-sized sheets with the headings above up on the wall. In your groups, you have five minutes to write your findings on each poster.

HEALTH ISSUES
(e.g. medical conditions such as high blood pressure)

LIFESTYLE FACTORS
(e.g. people who are forgetful might not want to use the pill)

BELIEFS AND VALUES
(e.g. belonging to a religious faith that does not allow contraception)

C. Discuss each poster as a class.

Condoms

Condoms (male) are thin latex tubes that cover the penis during sexual activity. They prevent semen and other fluids from coming into contact with the other person. They should be worn on the penis during vaginal, anal and oral sex. When used correctly, condoms give the best available protection against STI transmission. A new condom should be worn for every sexual act.

When there is a risk of pregnancy, it's advisable to combine condoms with another method of contraception (e.g. a hormonal contraception such as the pill) in order to have safer sex.

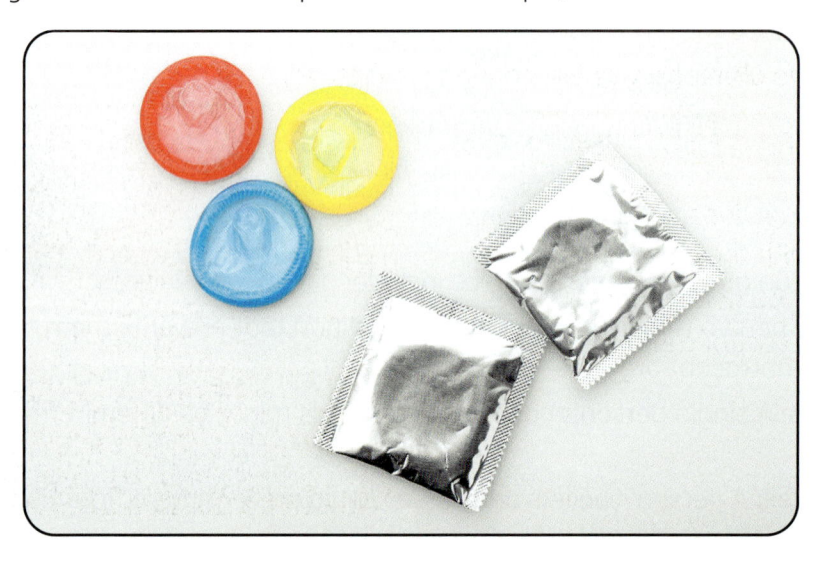

CHAPTER 30 – CONTRACEPTION: MAKING CHOICES

Here are some things that people should consider when using condoms:

Store condoms away from sunlight, check the expiry date on the pack, and look for the BSI Kitemark or CE mark that indicates the necessary safety testing.

⬆ BSI Kitemark   ⬆ CE mark

Carefully open the wrapper and remove the rolled-up condom. Jewellery and teeth can damage the condom, so it's best to push the condom to one side and rip the ridged edge of the wrapper.

To put on a condom: Pinch the tip of the condom to expel the air. While still pinching the tip, place the condom at the head of the penis and begin to unroll it down the shaft, all the way to the base. If the man has not been circumcised (foreskin removed for religious, cultural or medical reasons), then the foreskin would need to be gently pulled back as the condom is rolled down.

To reduce the risk of the condom breaking during sex, ensure there are minimal air bubbles.

Condoms should be removed shortly after sex, while the penis is still erect. The man wearing the condom should hold on to the base of it while pulling out of the vagina or anus. This will help prevent semen from leaking out and coming into contact with the other person.

Dispose of the used condom in a plastic bag and knot or seal the bag. Handwashing is important after handling used condoms.

ACTIVITY 30.3 – WATCH

A. Watch this video about how to use condoms effectively:

▶ www.educate*plus*.ie/go/using-condoms

B. Research the questions below and share your findings with the class.
 1. Where can you get condoms?
 2. What is the cost of them?

The withdrawal method

The **withdrawal method**, also known as 'pulling out', involves removing the penis from the vagina before ejaculation occurs. The goal of this method is to prevent sperm from entering the vagina.

The withdrawal method **is not** a form of contraception and **should not** be used as a method of birth control, as sperm may still enter the vagina if withdrawal isn't properly timed or if pre-ejaculation fluid contains sperm. The withdrawal method also doesn't offer protection against STIs.

ACTIVITY 30.4 – THINK

Take this quiz to recap what you have learned about contraception over the last two chapters.

	Statement	True	False
1	No method of contraception is 100% effective.		
2	Contraception is now free for everyone in Ireland.		
3	The withdrawal method is very reliable.		
4	Condoms can be reused.		
5	The vaginal ring is a small, flexible ring that is placed in the vagina.		
6	The mini pill contains oestrogen and progestogen.		

TIPS: A person can go to their GP or contact the sexual health centre for more information on contraception. Please note that some GPs may require the consent of a guardian before prescribing contraception to people under the age of 17.

? List three things that you learned about contraception in Ireland in this chapter.

Related Learning Outcomes: 3.5, 3.9

CHAPTER 31

STIs: Transmission and Types

In this chapter we will:
- learn the difference between STIs and STDs
- examine how STIs are transmitted
- research different types of STIs.

KEY TERMS
Sexually transmitted infection (STI)
Sexually transmitted disease (STD)
Asymptomatic

? Who is at risk of getting an STI?

The difference between STIs and STDs

A **sexually transmitted infection (STI)** is an infection that can be transmitted from one person to another through intimate contact. This means that someone with an STI can pass it on to another person during sexual activity. STIs broadly fit into three categories:

- viral
- bacterial
- parasitic.

More than 30 different bacteria, viruses and parasites are known to be transmitted through sexual contact, which includes vaginal, anal and oral sex. One of the highest risk groups for STIs is young people.

An STI becomes a **sexually transmitted disease (STD)** when it causes symptoms, leads to medical complications or starts affecting a person's health. For example, chlamydia may initially be an STI, but if left untreated, it can progress and cause pelvic inflammatory disease (PID) in women, making it an STD. Having an STI does not necessarily mean it will develop into a disease. It is possible to carry the infection and be contagious, yet never experience any symptoms or significant health issues.

ACTIVITY 31.1 – THINK

A. Read the statements about STIs in the table below. Indicate whether you think they are true or false. This activity can also be completed on the *You've Got This!* app.

	Statement	True	False
1	The rate of STIs rose by more than 75% in 2023.		
2	Gonorrhoea rates have increased by 25% and chlamydia rates have increased by 10% between 2019 and 2022.		
3	STIs are common, particularly chlamydia, herpes and gonorrhoea.		
4	In 2022, the group most affected by STIs were young people aged 15 to 24 years.		
5	A fifth of all STIs reported in 2022 were in people aged under 25 years of age.		
6	The symptoms of STIs are sometimes not noticed.		
7	You can only have one STI at a time.		
8	You can't get an STI the first time you have sex.		
9	Hygienic people are not likely to get an STI.		
10	All STIs can be cured.		

B. Reflection questions:
1. Of the true statements, which one surprised you the most? Why?
2. Of the true statements, which one made you the most anxious? Why?
3. Did any of the facts reassure you?

Transmission of STIs

STIs can be contracted and transferred regardless of sexual orientation, age or gender. A person who has an STI can pass it on to another person without even realising. Unprotected sexual contact can put you at risk of contracting STIs, as they are transmitted through infected blood, semen and vaginal fluids. You do not need to have penetrative sex to get an STI.

STIs can sometimes be transmitted non-sexually. Mothers can pass STIs on to their infants during pregnancy or childbirth, or while breastfeeding. STIs can also be spread through blood transfusions or shared needles. Parasites such as pubic lice can be contracted through infected bed linen.

When sexually active people use condoms, limit their number of sexual partners and become aware of STIs, they reduce the risk of contracting or transmitting STIs.

Many STIs can be **asymptomatic**, which means that they don't have noticeable symptoms or signs of infection. Because of this, regular sexual health check-ups are important for sexually active people. Be aware that asymptomatic STIs are not necessarily harmless. Chlamydia, for example, can be asymptomatic but may lead to problems with fertility.

If symptoms are observed, seeking early medical advice is crucial. Correct and immediate diagnosis and treatment can lead to many STIs being cured completely, while all STIs can be treated to minimise their impact on overall health.

CHAPTER 31 – STIS: TRANSMISSION AND TYPES

STI facts:
- ✓ You can get an STI even if you know your partner.
- ✓ You can't tell if someone has an STI by looking at them.
- ✓ You can get STIs from oral sex.
- ✓ You can be infected with more than one STI at a time.
- ✓ You can get an STI more than once.

ACTIVITY 31.2 – DISCUSS

A. In groups, use these reliable sources to research the 15 different types of STIs in the table below:

www.educate*plus*.ie/go/sexualwellbeing-STIs

www.educate*plus*.ie/go/human-papilloma-virus-hpv

Bacterial vaginosis (BV)	Chlamydia	Genital herpes (HSV)
Genital warts (HPV)	Gonorrhoea	Hepatitis B
HIV	Molluscum contagiosum	Pelvic inflammatory disease (PID)
Pubic lice (crabs)	Scabies	Syphilis
Thrush	Trichomonas vaginalis (TV)	Human papillomavirus (HPV)

B. Your teacher will put five posters up on the wall. Each poster will have three of the STIs above on them, with spaces to answer these questions:

1. What is it?
2. How would I get it?
3. What symptoms would I have?
4. How is it treated?

For example:

BACTERIAL VAGINOSIS (BV)
What is it?
How would I get it?
What symptoms would I have?
How is it treated?

CHLAMYDIA
What is it?
How would I get it?
What symptoms would I have?
How is it treated?

GENITAL HERPES (HSV)
What is it?
How would I get it?
What symptoms would I have?
How is it treated?

C. Your group will have five minutes at each poster to fill in as much information as you can. When your time is up, move on to the next poster and fill in any information that the other groups haven't included. Continue this until all the posters have been filled in.

D. Discuss each poster as a class.

YOU'VE GOT THIS! 3 – THIRD YEAR SPHE

👥 ACTIVITY 31.3 – READ

In groups, read these three case studies and answer the questions that follow. You can refer to the posters created in Activity 31.2 to help you.

Case study 1

Brandon decides to visit an STI clinic because he notices considerable pain and swelling in both of his testicles. He feels worried because he recently had sex without a condom.

1. What STI might Brandon have?
2. Is it bacterial, viral or parasitic?
3. What could happen if not treated?
4. How is it passed on?
5. How would it be diagnosed?
6. What is the likely treatment?
7. What advice would you give him about reducing the risk of future infection?

Case study 2

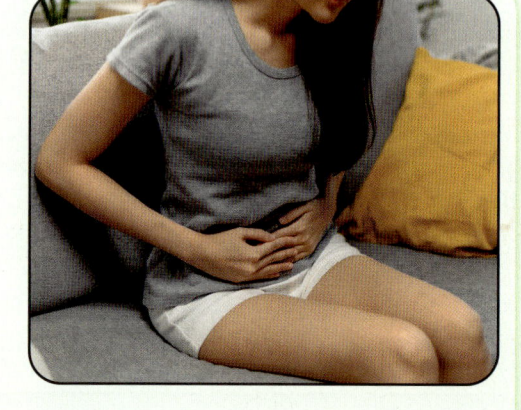

Amanda is considering going to an STI clinic, but feels awkward and embarrassed about doing so. Her symptoms include abnormal vaginal discharge and a pain in her stomach that has resulted in diarrhoea. She has recently entered a new relationship and hasn't always used condoms during sex.

1. What STI might Amanda have?
2. Is it bacterial, viral or parasitic?
3. What could happen if not treated?
4. How is it passed on?
5. How would it be diagnosed?
6. What is the likely treatment?
7. What advice would you give her about reducing the risk of future infection?

Case study 3

Gregory wants to speak with his GP. His genitals are very itchy, and he has developed severe scratch marks from scratching them. He has also recently noticed some black spots on his underwear.

1. What STI might Gregory have?
2. Is it bacterial, viral or parasitic?
3. What could happen if not treated?
4. How is it passed on?
5. How would it be diagnosed?
6. What is the likely treatment?
7. What advice would you give him about reducing the risk of future infection?

CHAPTER 31 – STIS: TRANSMISSION AND TYPES

ACTIVITY 31.4 – CREATE

Create an information leaflet on an STI of your choice. The leaflet can be created digitally or in a physical format, and should include the following headings:

- What is it?
- How does a person get it?
- What are the symptoms?
- Diagnosis
- Transmission
- Prevention
- Where to go for testing

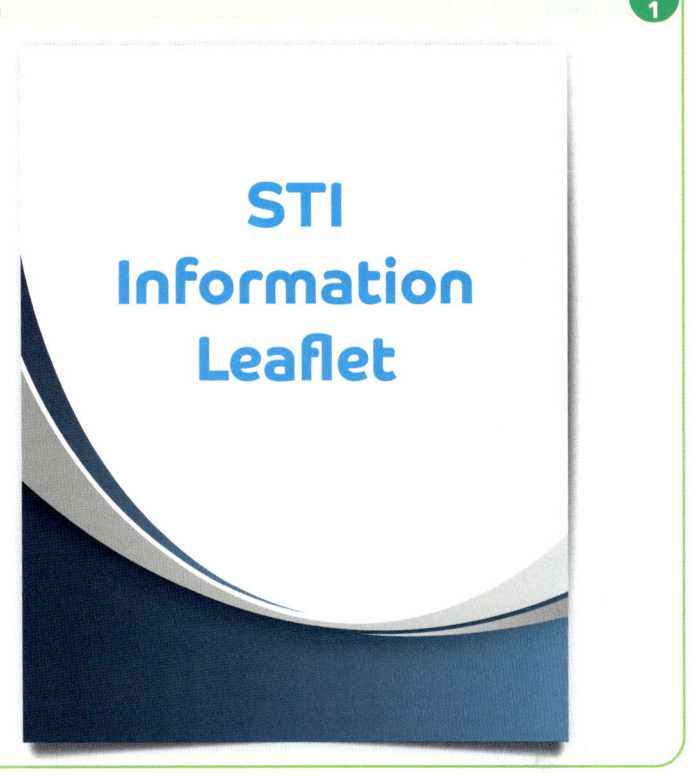

STI Information Leaflet

TIPS

- People should always use a condom when having any sexual contact.
- It is important to visit a GP or an STI clinic to access treatment for an STI.
- People should be honest about their sexual health and discuss potential STIs with a partner.
- Getting regular sexual health check-ups is necessary for good reproductive health.

? What advice would you give someone who is worried about STIs?

Related Learning Outcomes: 3.5, 3.9, 3.11.

CHAPTER 32

STIs: Testing and Treatment

In this chapter we will:
- discuss how STIs can be tested for
- investigate how STIs can be treated.

KEY TERMS
Swab
Human Immunodeficiency Virus (HIV)

❓ How does a sexually active person reduce the risk of getting an STI?

STI testing

If a person has any symptoms that indicate that they might have an STI, they should seek professional advice from their GP, a pharmacist or an STI clinic so that a test can be arranged. If a person has no symptoms, and they are over the age of 17, they have the option to undergo a free home STI test. As it's possible to have an STI without being aware of it, undergoing testing is essential.

The age of sexual consent in Ireland is 17 years. If you're over 16, you can consent to medical treatment, including any treatment or tests needed for an STI. The type of test will depend on the kind of sexual contact and whether there are symptoms. The test could involve:

- giving a urine sample in a small bottle
- a **swab** (an absorbent tool like a cotton bud) being taken from inside of the tip of the penis
- a swab being taken from the throat or anus
- a swab being taken from the vagina
- blood being taken to check for HIV, syphilis and sometimes Hepatitis B and C.

The procedure will be explained by the healthcare professional. It's always a good idea to communicate with your partner if you have an STI so they can be tested and treated if necessary.

CHAPTER 32 – STIS: TESTING AND TREATMENT

ACTIVITY 32.1 – WATCH

Free home STI testing kits are available for people over the age of 17. Watch this video about the national testing service and answer the questions that follow.

▶ www.educate*plus*.ie/go/STI-home-kit

1. Where can someone over the age of 17 access the testing kit?
2. How much does it cost?
3. What is in the kit?
4. What should the person do to ensure safety before using the lancet needle?
5. How long do the results take?

STI treatment

STI testing and treatment is free in public STI clinics. The type of treatment will depend on the STI a person has. For example, antibiotics are used to treat bacterial STIs, and antiviral medications are used to treat viral STIs, depending on the STI.

There are several HPV vaccines that target and provide protection against many strains of Human Papillomavirus (HPV), which is a very common group of viruses transmitted through sexual contact. The most commonly used HPV vaccines are Gardasil and Cervarix.

While all STIs can be treated, not all of them can be cured.

ACTIVITY 32.2 – READ

In pairs, read these scenarios. For each one, imagine the main character is asking you for advice. What would you tell them?

Scenario 1
Jonathan has just learned that he has an STI. He wants to tell his partner, but is afraid of what his partner will think.

Scenario 2
Donal has never had sex. He recently shared needles with friends at a tattooing party, and has now realised that he put himself at risk for contracting HIV, Hepatitis B and Hepatitis C. He is worried.

Scenario 3
Lorraine is not in a relationship. She sometimes has casual dates involving sexual contact. She is worried about STIs and wants to know how to recognise the symptoms.

Scenario 4
Joanne has been dating the same person for eight months. When they first had sex, they used condoms. However, they stopped using them about a month ago. Recently, Joanne noticed small, itchy bumps on her genitals.

Scenario 5
Shawn has been with the same partner for two years and just tested positive for chlamydia.

ACTIVITY 32.3 – READ

Read this case study and answer the questions that follow.

Case study

After noticing some vaginal discharge and pain passing urine, Laoise was diagnosed with chlamydia. At first, she was shocked, embarrassed and angry. She'd only ever had sex with one person – her boyfriend, who had said that she was his first sexual partner. It hadn't crossed her mind to talk to him about getting tested. In her opinion, they had been really safe, using condoms most of the time.

Now she realises that the choices she made could affect the rest of her life. The doctor told her that despite receiving treatment, she may experience fertility problems (trouble getting pregnant) later in life due to how advanced her infection is.

1. Do you think that Laoise had a clear understanding of STI transmission before her diagnosis?
2. What emotional impact do you think the diagnosis has had on Laoise?
3. What lessons can we learn from Laoise's story about the importance of communication in sexual relationships?
4. How might Laoise's experience impact her future sexual relationships and practices?
5. How might Laoise's story influence your own decisions and attitudes toward sexual health and safety?

HIV

Human Immunodeficiency Virus (HIV) is an infection that attacks the body's immune system. If it's not treated, it can lead to Acquired Immunodeficiency Syndrome (AIDS). HIV can be acquired through sexual contact, blood to blood contact, and during pregnancy and breastfeeding. It was once untreatable, and as a result there is still a stigma attached to HIV as being a life-ending condition. However, while HIV can't be cured, there are now effective treatments available for people diagnosed with HIV, allowing them to live full, healthy lives.

HIV prevention

Condoms can prevent people from acquiring HIV when used correctly and consistently. There are also two preventative measures for people who may have come into contact with HIV or are vulnerable to acquiring HIV:

> **PEP (post-exposure prophylaxis)** is a short-term course of medication that a person takes after a recent exposure to HIV. The medication stops the virus from establishing itself in the body. It must be started within 72 hours of a potential exposure to HIV.

> **PrEP (pre-exposure prophylaxis)** is medication that is taken by a person who doesn't have HIV to prevent them from acquiring the virus. It is extremely effective at preventing people from acquiring HIV through sexual contact.

HIV treatment

Antiviral medicines are used to treat people who have HIV. These medicines are taken every day and work by stopping the virus from replicating in the body. This allows the immune system to repair itself and prevents further damage.

HIV treatment can lead to an undetectable viral load, which means that the amount of HIV in the body is very low and it can't be passed on to sexual partners. Therefore, accessing medication and taking it as directed means that there is no risk of HIV being passed on. HIV treatment is free in Ireland.

ACTIVITY 32.4 – READ

Read this case study and answer the questions that follow.

Case study

Ruairí was diagnosed with HIV during a routine health check-up. He was initially shocked and anxious, because he was worried about what this meant for his wellbeing. He initially believed that his health was in danger and that he would not be able to treat his diagnosis. He also felt scared to tell his family and friends about it.

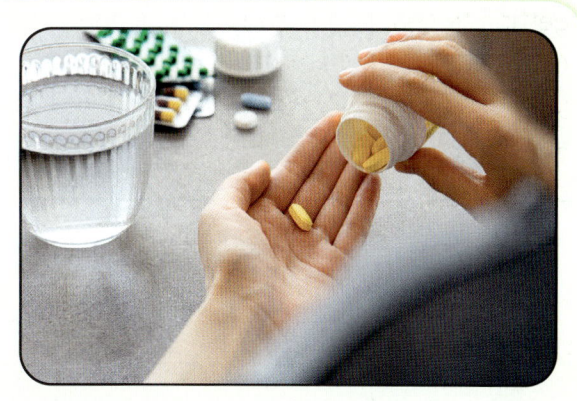

However, despite these feelings, Ruairí decided to be proactive about managing his condition. He spoke to his doctor about his treatment options, and was prescribed antiviral medication to control the virus and boost his immune system. Ruairí also did some research on HIV to help clear up any myths he believed about it. Doing this helped reduce his fear about his condition.

1. How did the HIV diagnosis initially affect Ruairí's emotional wellbeing?
2. Why do you think Ruairí felt scared to tell his family and friends about it?
3. How did Ruairí choose to respond to the diagnosis?
4. Why do you think there is a stigma attached to being HIV positive?

ACTIVITY 32.5 – CREATE

In groups, create a presentation to educate other students about STIs. The presentation should include:

- three or more facts about STIs that all teenagers need to know
- three or more possible symptoms of STIs
- reasons why it's important to talk about STIs with any potential sexual partner
- reasons why it's important to speak with a doctor about safer sexual activity
- three or more resources that students can turn to for reliable information and testing (trusted adults, medical professionals, clinics or hotlines).

ACTIVITY 32.6 – THINK

Take this quiz to recap what you have learned about STIs over the last two chapters.

1. List five STIs.
2. List the three categories that STIs fall under.
3. Can someone have an STI and not know? Why?
4. What type of drugs are used to cure bacterial STIs?
5. How are viral STIs treated?
6. Name one STI that can be tested for using a blood sample.
7. Can someone have more than one STI at the same time?
8. What vaccine protects against many strains of HPV?
9. What type of contraception offers the best available protection against STIs?
10. List three places where people can access STI tests.

TIPS

- STIs are mainly spread through sexual contact, including vaginal, anal and oral sex. Awareness is the first step in prevention.
- Using condoms consistently and correctly during sexual activity is very important.
- If you suspect you may have an STI or have symptoms, consult a healthcare professional such as your GP, a pharmacist or an STI clinic for testing and treatment, if needed. Here is a list of public STI clinics: www.educateplus.ie/go/HSE-STI-services
- People over the age of 17 in Ireland can access a free home STI test from www.SH24.ie.
- Open and honest communication is crucial in maintaining sexual health.

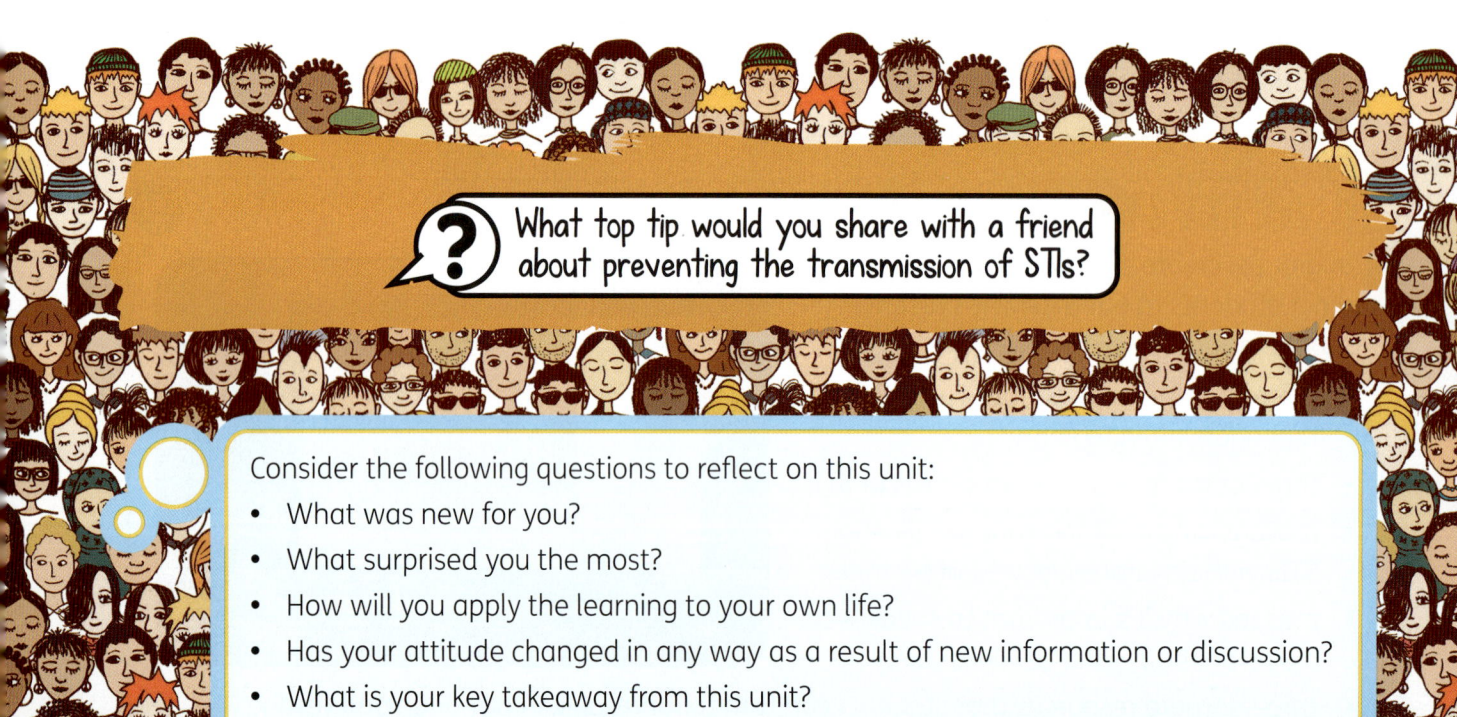

? What top tip would you share with a friend about preventing the transmission of STIs?

Consider the following questions to reflect on this unit:
- What was new for you?
- What surprised you the most?
- How will you apply the learning to your own life?
- Has your attitude changed in any way as a result of new information or discussion?
- What is your key takeaway from this unit?
- If you were to do a project on this topic, what would you like to learn more about?

Notes

Notes